# Be the Barista

First Edition: October 2015

Author: Seungmin Ryu
Publisher: Mangon Kang
Editors: Hanghyun Jo, Jeonghyeon Park
Designer: Kangseop Yang
Photos: Fine Studio

Publishing Company: Yeoreum Communication
Address: 13, Yongsan 1-gil, Deokjin-gu, Jeonju-si, Jeollabuk-do, Korea, 54933
Telephone: +82-63-273-5771
Fax: +82-63-273-5172
www.yeoreum.com



○
초　판 | 2015년 10월
●
지은이 | 유승민
펴낸이 | 강만곤
주　간 | 조항현, 박정현
디자인 | 양강섭
사　진 | 파인스튜디오
●
펴낸곳 | 여름커뮤니케이션
주　소 | 54933 전라북도 전주시 덕진구 용산1길 13
전　화 | 063) 273-5771
팩　스 | 063) 273-5172
www.yeoreum.com



값 25,000원

**ISBN** 978-89-963924-9-1 (13570)

# 나도 바리스타

# Be the Barista

# Introduction
# 서문

You may have had times when you were confused by the menus at a coffee shop. Some coffee beverages may have different names depending on the coffee shop even though they use the same ingredients. When another ingredient is added, the menu will have a different name again. So don't be embarrassed at not understanding confusing names on the menu. There is no absolute rule for naming.

This book introduces various ingredients, how to make them, and even the selection of right cups or glasses for each menu item. What I wish is that this book will be able to inspire you to create your own names or recipes for menus.

While I give lectures to audiences at schools or associations, I often see some people who strictly follow existing ways of making coffee beverages. I assume that they have learned about coffee from books or courses that were defining what "coffee" is, and sincerely followed it.

There is nothing wrong if you grind whole beans and enjoy it as as you want, even though some people say that you should not add sugar to espresso.

Coffees do not have a right single answer. Create your own coffees and enjoy them. Coffee pleases us only with its flavors. If there is a right answer for a good coffee, it will be the coffee that you make and like.

Professor Seungmin Ryu
Department of Coffee, Kunjang University College

커피전문점에서 커피 메뉴판을 보는 순간 당황스러운 경험을 가진 경우가 많이 있을 것이다. 똑같은 재료를 사용하여 만든 커피음료라도 커피전문점마다 메뉴명이 다를 수가 있고, 여기에 부재료 하나 조금 추가하여 메뉴명이 달라지기도 한다. 커피전문점에서 사용하는 메뉴명이 절대적이지 않다는 것을 알았으면 하고, 메뉴 이름에 너무 신경을 쓰지 않았으면 하는 생각이다.

이 책에 소개된 메뉴 레시피의 재료, 만드는 과정, 잔의 선택 등을 참고로 하여 독자 여러분들께서 부재료들을 추가하거나 제외하여 자신만의 독창적인 메뉴를 만들거나 메뉴 이름을 다양하게 가져갈 수 있도록 하는 것이 이 필자의 바램이다.

학교나 단체에서 커피강의를 하면서 느낀 점이 기존의 커피 메뉴를 만드는 방식만 고집하는 사람들을 종종 보게 된다. 이것은 아마도 "커피는 이것이다"라고 안내 해놓은 서적이나 교육과정에서 배운 것을 그대로 따르는 것이 정도라 생각하기 때문 일 것이다.

커피를 분쇄하여 인스턴트커피처럼 타서 즐긴다고 해서 잘못된 것이 아니다. 그리고 에스프레소에 설탕을 넣어 마시면 안 되는 것처럼 이야기하는 사람도 있다.

커피에는 정답이 없다. 창의적인 자신만의 커피세계를 만들었으면 좋겠다. 커피는 향기만으로도 우리를 즐겁게 하는 음료다. "내가 만들고, 내가 좋아하는 커피가 정답"일 것이다.

군장대학교 커피학과 교수

유 승 민

# Contents

Exploring Coffee Menus

# 커피메뉴 들여다 보기

# Coffee menu

## How Can I Find and Order What I Want?

It is often confusing to find and order something from coffee menus at a coffee shop. You just want a cup of coffee, but what they say is too fancy and even in foreign languages.

Coffee menus are mostly in Italian and French because they have been created and developed in Europe.

Even when using the same ingredients, some coffee beverages have different names depending on the coffee shop. In particular, when a coffee shop creates a coffee beverage with an original recipe, they will give it their own name. Like this, brewed coffee may have various menus depending on additional ingredients or methods used.

You do not need to feel embarrassed if you do not understand what the coffee menu describes. Ask your barista or serving staff. Then, you will get what you want with no regrets.

## 커피메뉴 주문은 어떻게 해야 하나?

커피전문점에서 커피메뉴판을 보고 주문을 하려고 하면 당혹스러운 경우가 많다. 메뉴판에 외국어만 가득하여 그 메뉴가 그 메뉴 같고, "그냥 커피"는 찾아 볼 수가 없어 난감하다.

커피메뉴 이름이 대부분 이탈리아, 프랑스어로 구성된 것은 커피음료가 유럽을 중심으로 발전했기 때문이다. 여기에 영어까지 섞여 커피메뉴 이름이 낯설기만 하다. 커피음료는 동일한 재료를 사용하더라도 각 커피전문점마다 메뉴 이름이 다른 경우가 많다. 재료는 비슷하지만 자체적으로 개발하여 커피전문점만의 이름을 붙인다. 이처럼 추출된 커피에 어떤 부재료와 만드는 방식에 따라 새로운 메뉴의 이름이 지어진다.

커피를 주문할 때 잘 모르는 메뉴에 대해서는 미안하게 생각하지 말고 직원들에게 상세하게 물어보자. 그래야 후회하지 않는다.

# Brewing Devices for Coffee Menus

## 커피메뉴를 위한 추출 기구

Semi-automatic espresso machine
에스프레소 반자동 머신

Full-automatic espresso machine
에스프레소 전자동 머신

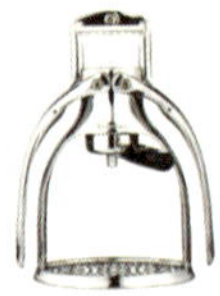

Handpress
핸드프레스

Coffee maker
커피메이커

Drippers and servers
드립퍼와 서버

Siphon
사이폰

French press
프레치프레스

Moka pot
모카포트

Cezve
체즈베

Cafe phin
카페핀

Dutch coffee brewer
더치추출 기구

Commercial grinder
상업용 그라인더

Grinder for home use
가정용 그라인더

Hand mill
핸드밀

Thermometer
온도계

PRESSO

Kalita.

Blender
블렌더

Shaker
쉐이커

Measuring cup
계량컵

Cream whipper
휘핑기

Steam pitcher
스팀피처

Foam maker
거품기

Squeezer
스퀴저

Milk spoon
우유스푼

Decorator
데코레이터

Induction cooker
인덕션

Ice machine
제빙기

Various glasses and cups
각종 글라스와 컵

# Ingredients of Coffee Menus

Basic coffee ingredients include coffee, water, sugar, and milk. Other ingredients can be added to create a variety of coffee menus.

## 1. Coffee

### Single-Origin Coffees

Single-origin coffees are grown in the same geographical area. These coffees can be used to for their unique flavors and tastes. Single-origin coffees are usually brewed using drippers.

### Blend Coffees

When you mix two or more coffees with different origins or different degree, it is called blend coffee which creates unique tastes and flavors.

The brewed blend coffee by an espresso machine is often used for variation menus.

## 2. Other Ingredients

### Milk

### Syrup

Syrup usually refers to something made of fruit with added sugar. As for coffee recipes, syrup is considered as a liquid additive containing artificial flavors, for example, chocolate, vanilla, sugar, or caramel syrup.

### Sauce

A sauce is a liquid or semi-solid condiment poured over food to enhance its taste or color. In general, various kinds of sauces are made by processing natural ingredients to puree, which can be used with other seasonings, and served with various dishes as the type of topping or sauce. In coffee recipes, caramel, chocolate or vanilla sauce is often used. It is usually added to a cup of coffee, but sometimes it is used on the top of whipped cream for decoration.

### Ice

Ice is one of basic ingredients in coffee recipes. You can put ice cubes into a glass or a small bowl, and shake ice with other ingredients to make iced coffee menus.

## 커피메뉴의 재료

커피의 가장 기본적인 재료들은 커피, 설탕, 우유라고 할 수 있다. 여기에 부재료들을 첨가하면 새로운 메뉴들이 탄생한다.

### 1. 커피

**단품(단종)**
각 나라 및 지역별 단품으로 그 나라의 커피특성(개성)이나 특징을 살릴 수 있다. 주로 드립커피로 추출하는 메뉴에 사용한다.

**블렌딩(혼합)**
산지나 로스팅 정도가 다른 두 종류 이상의 단품 원두를 적절히 혼합하여 독특한 맛과 향을 지닌 새로운 커피로 만들어 내는 것을 블렌딩 커피라 한다.
에스프레소 머신으로 추출하여 베리에이션(Variation) 메뉴에 주로 사용된다.

### 2. 부재료

**우유(Milk)**

**시럽(Syrup)**
보통 시럽은 과일즙에 설탕을 가한 과일시럽(Fruits syrup)을 말하는데 커피에서는 대부분 캐러멜, 바닐라 등 인공향료를 첨가한 식품첨가물의 액상이다. 초코시럽, 바닐라시럽, 설탕시럽, 캐러멜시럽 등이 사용된다.

**소스(Sauce)**
서양요리에서 맛이나 빛깔을 내기 위하여 식품에 넣거나 위에 껴얹는 액체 조미료의 총칭으로 커피메뉴에 같이 넣기도 하지만 휘핑크림 위에 모양을 내기 위한 토핑용으로 많이 사용한다.
소스는 천연재료를 퓨레(Puree)의 형태로 가공해서 설탕이나 각종 양념류 등을 첨가 후 조리하여 요리에 얹어 먹거나 찍어 먹는 형태이다.
커피메뉴에서는 캐러멜소스(Caramel Sauce), 초콜릿소스(Chocolate Sauce), 바닐라소스(Vanilla Sauce) 등이 있다.

**얼음**
얼음은 아이스커피(Ice Coffee) 메뉴의 기본으로 덩어리 얼음을 직접 사용하거나 셰이킹 할 때 사용한다.

# Selecting a Right Method for Coffee Menu

## 1. Coffee Menus based on How to Use Whole Beans

Coffee menus can vary depending on whether you want to use single-origin or blend coffees.

### Straight Coffee

Most straight coffees use single-origin coffees with soluble components, keeping unique flavors and tastes of their origins.

### Variation

Blend coffees are used to create variations with balanced tastes and flavors. These coffees are brewed using the pressure extraction of espresso machine.

## 2. Coffee Menus based on How to Brew Coffees

### Coffees Brewed by an Espresso Machine (Pressurized Brewing)

Pressurized brewing, which extracts fat-soluble and water-soluble compounds at the same time, gives coffee a strong body. This method is appropriate for variation menus using other ingredients including milk, heavy cream, or syrup.

### Coffees Brewed by Natural Pressure

Drip brewing using natural pressure is good for straight coffees. Other ingredients may be added depending on personal preferences. This method usually creates a light and neat taste because drippers tend to brew water-soluble compounds much more than fat-soluble compounds.

## 커피메뉴 조리 방식의 선택

### 1. 원두 사용에 따른 메뉴 구성

커피메뉴는 원두커피를 단품커피로 할 것인가 블렌딩(혼합)커피로 할 것인가에 따라 메뉴가 각각 달라진다.

**스트레이트 커피(Straight)**
각 나라별 커피의 특성이나 개성을 살린 수용성 성분의 단품커피를 사용한다.

**베리에이션(Variation)**
균형 잡힌 맛을 내기 위한 블렌딩커피를 사용하고 에스프레소머신으로 가압추출한다.

### 2. 추출방법에 따른 메뉴 구성

**에스프레소 머신(가압)으로 추출한 커피**
커피머신으로 추출한 커피는 지용성(Crema)과 수용성 성분을 추출하게 되어 강한 바디감으로 부재료(우유, 생크림, 시럽 등)를 사용한 베리에이션 메뉴 사용에 적합하다.

**자연압으로 추출한 커피**
드립(자연압)으로 추출하여 스트레이트(Straight)로 커피를 즐기기에 적합하다. 물론 기호에 따라 부재료를 추가할 수도 있다. 자연압으로 추출할 경우에는 드립퍼에 따라 지용성 성분보다는 대부분 수용성 성분이 추출되어 맛이 깔끔하다.

## Espresso

To enjoy espresso, which means "express" in English, you need to grind whole beans, compress the coffee grounds, and quickly let water pass through the compressed the grounds using steam pressure. Baristas may have different preferences on how to brew espresso, but it is recommended to include 7 to 8 grams (+/–0.5g ) of coffee, set the water pressure at 9 bar (about 8 to 10 bar), extract for 20 to 30 seconds, 30 ml (25 to 30 ml) of brewed coffee, and a 92°C (about 90 to 95°C) brewing temperature.

## ● 에스프레소(Espresso)

에스프레소는 영어로 "Express(빠르다)"에서 유래되었다. 분쇄되어 압축된 커피가루에 증기압력으로 물을 신속하게 투과시켜 추출한 커피다. 에스프레소의 기준은 바리스타마다 차이는 있지만 커피 투입량은 7~8g(±0.5g), 추출되는 물의 압력은 9bar(약 8~10bar), 추출시간은 20~30초(약 25초), 추출량은 30ml(25~30ml), 추출온도는 92℃(약 90~95℃)의 범위 내에서 추출하면 최상의 에스프레소를 추출할 수 있다.

## How to Make Espresso
### 에스프레소 추출 순서

Prepare cups.
잔 준비하기

Separate the portafilter.
포터필터 뽑기

Drain water.
물 흘려 버리기

Clean the filter basket.
필터 바스켓 닦기

Fill the basket with ground coffee.
바스켓에 분쇄커피 채우기

Level the ground coffee.
고르기

Compact the ground coffee with a tamper.
누르기

Shake the rim.
가장자리 털기

Install the portafilter.
포터필터 장착하기

Press the brewing button.
추출버튼 누르기

Take off the portafilter.
포터필터 뽑기

Rinse with running water.
물 흘려 버리기

Remove cookies.
쿠키 버리기

Washing the Filter Holder
필터홀더 닦기

Install the portafilter back.
포터필터 채워두기

Espresso
에스프레소

## Basic Terms for Coffee Menus

### Café or Caffè

Since this term refers to coffee, this term is supposed to come at the beginning of coffee menus such as americano and macchiato, but often omitted.

### Latte

Latte refers to milk.

### Variation

It refers to coffee menus made with other ingredients like milk or syrup. For instance, you can make caffè caramel latte with espresso, milk, and caramel syrup.

### Shot

It refers to a shot of espresso. One shot is 30 ml.

## 메뉴의 기본적인 용어

### 카페(Cafè)

'카페'는 커피를 의미하는 것이기 때문에 커피메뉴 앞에 카페를 붙이는 것이 원칙이다. 카페 아메리카노, 카페 마끼아또 등과 같이 앞에 카페를 붙이는 것이 정상인데 일반적으로 줄여서 부르고 있다.

### 라떼(Lattè)

라떼는 우유를 뜻한다.

### 베리에이션(Variation)

커피에 우유, 시럽 등 부재료를 첨가하여 만드는 메뉴(예, 에스프레소+우유+캐러멜시럽 = 캐러멜라떼)이다.

### 샷(Shot)

샷은 에스프레소의 샷을 의미하고 1샷은 30ml이다.

## Basic Terms of Espresso

| | |
|---|---|
| **Solo** | A shot of espresso |
| **Dopio** | Double solos, that is, double espresso |
| **Lungo** | Espresso that was over extracted for about 40 seconds |
| **Ristretto** | Espresso brewed in a very short time (about 15 seconds). Once the strongest flavor is reached, stop brewing the coffee. |

## 에스프레소(Espresso)의 기본 용어

| | |
|---|---|
| **솔로**(Solo) | 한 잔의 에스프레소(에스프레소와 동일) |
| **도피오**(Dopio) | 솔로의 두 배 즉 더블 에스프레소(Double Espresso) |
| **룽고**(Lungo) | 에스프레소를 길게 뽑은 것, 과다 추출한 것(일반적으로 40초 정도 추출) |
| **리스트레또**(Restretto) | 에스프레소를 아주 짧게(15초 정도) 추출한 것(가장 진한 시점에서 추출을 멈춘다.) |

## Mocha

The term Mocha can be added to all coffee menus using chocolate syrup. This name is associated with the chocolate flavor of coffees produced in Yemen and Ethiopia. In fact, Mocha was the name of renowned trade port in Yemen.

Based on this background, coffee shops began to put this term in drinks that have chocolate flavors. When dark chocolate is used in a coffee menu, it is called Mocha coffee. When white chocolate is used, it will be called white Mocha coffee.

## Terms for Coffee Menus using Espresso

Coffee menus based on espresso are normally in Italian, which is the origin of espresso. The names of espresso menus also involve the features of ingredients or styles.

| | |
|---|---|
| **Café / Caffè** | coffee |
| **Latte** | milk |
| **Panna** | Cream |
| **Mocha** | Chocolate |
| **Macchiato** | Mark |
| **Affogatoto** | dip, or to pour, etc. |

Ex. Caffè latter, which means coffee and milk, is an espresso menu with milk added.

## 모카(Mocha)

모카는 초콜릿시럽을 첨가한 메뉴의 통칭으로 사용된다. 예멘과 에티오피아에서 생산되는 커피의 초콜릿향과 연관있다. 모카는 옛날 유명했던 예멘의 커피 무역항 이름이다.

커피전문점에서 '모카'라는 이름이 붙여 사용하는 것은 초콜릿 향미가 나는 커피에서 착안한 것이다. 커피에 직접 초콜릿을 첨가해서 '모카'라는 메뉴 이름이 탄생하였다. 다크(Dark) 초콜릿을 사용하느냐 아니면 화이트(White) 초콜릿을 사용하느냐에 따라서 모카커피 혹은 화이트모카커피가 된다.

## 에스프레소로 만든 커피메뉴에 사용되는 단어들

에스프레소로 만들어지는 커피메뉴의 이름은 주로 이탈리아어다. 에스프레소의 출생지이기 때문이다. 에스프레소에 첨가되는 재료나 스타일에 따라 커피메뉴 이름에 붙여진다.

| | |
|---|---|
| **카페**(Cafè) | 커피(Coffee) |
| **라떼**(Latte) | 우유(Milk) |
| **판나**(Panna) | 크림(Cream) |
| **모카**(Mocha) | 초콜릿(Chocolate) |
| **마끼아또**(Machiato) | 마크(Mark) |
| **아포가토**(Affogato) | 빠지다, 끼얹다 등등 |

예) **카페라떼**(Cafe Latte)는 커피와 우유로 에스프레소에 우유를 첨가한 것이다.

## Regular Coffee, a Basic of Coffee Menu

### Americano or American Style

Americano can be said to be an American-style brewed coffee, which is thin like drip coffee. This coffee originated from American people's life style, in which a lot of thin coffee is brewed and enjoyed all day long.

### Regular Coffee

A regular coffee usually means a medium-sized coffee, but it also refers to drip coffee that has no additional ingredients other than water. Customers use expressions like "strong", "weak", "or "regular" to indicate their desired strength of coffee. In South Korea, it refers to diluted coffee with some sugar added.

### Black Coffee

This term refers to coffee without any other ingredients: no sugar or syrup.

## 커피메뉴의 기본인 레귤러커피(Regular Coffee)

### 아메리카노(Americano), 혹은 아메리칸 스타일(American Style)

통상적으로 말하는 커피는 말 그대로 미국식 드립커피다. 미국인들은 대부분 커피를 연하게 추출해서 옆에 두고 천천히 조금씩 즐기는 문화에서 유래되었다. 양이 많고 연한 드립형 원두커피다.

### 레귤러커피(Regular Coffee)

레귤러의 뜻은 보통 사이즈의 커피를 말하는데 통상적으로 다른 부재료가 들어가지 않는다. 물로 희석한 모든 추출 커피류의 총칭으로 진하게, 연하게, 적당하게로 주문한다.

### 블랙커피(Black Coffee)

커피에 설탕이나 시럽 등 아무것도 넣지 않은 커피를 의미한다.

### 하우스 블렌드(House Blend)

커피 로스팅업체나 커피전문점 자체적으로 자기만의 노하우로 볶은 커피를 블렌딩한 것이다.

## Naming Coffee Menus by Syrup or Sauce

When a syrup or sauce with vanilla, caramel, or hazelnut flavor is used in the recipe of a coffee menu, it will be also added in the name of the coffee menu.

For instance, when a vanilla, caramel, or hazelnut flavor is added to latte menus, they will be named as vanilla, caramel, or hazelnut latte respectively. Thus, the names of coffee menus are diversified. The difference between latte and cappuccino is the amount of milk and milk foam per 1 oz of espresso.

## 시럽(Syrup)이나 소스(Source) 첨가에 따른 메뉴의 분류

시럽이나 소스 즉, 바닐라(Vanilla), 캐러멜(Caramel), 헤이즐넛(Hazelnut) 등이 첨가된 메뉴는 그 시럽의 이름이 커피메뉴에 붙여진다.

예) 해당 시럽이나 소스가 들어간 메뉴의 이름으로 바닐라라떼, 캐러멜라떼, 헤이즐넛라떼 등이 있다. 이런 방식으로 이름이 붙여지고 다양한 메뉴로 늘어나게 된다. 라떼(Latte)와 카푸치노(Cappuccino)의 차이는 에스프레소 1온스에 우유와 우유거품량의 차이다.

## Terms of Iced Coffee Menus

Iced coffee refers to all kinds of drinks made with coffee and ice. Like hot coffee menus, there are a variety of iced coffee variants depending on the ingredients, coffee shops, and countries. These menus also may have different names by country.

**Frappe**
A French word that refers to a cold drink with ice

**Freddo**
An Italian word that refers to iced drinks with foam. The foam is created by shaking ingredients including ice, espresso, cold water, and sugar syrup

**Shakerrato**
An Italian word for "shaker," referring to a drink made by shaking ice, sugar, and espresso together

**Granita**
A semi-frozen dessert made from fruit, sugar and wine

**Shaker**
A container used to mix ingredients, specifically to serve cold coffee. Ice and coffee are put in together and shaken. Only the coffee is poured out to be served.

## ● 아이스커피(Iced Coffee) 메뉴의 용어

아이스커피는 에스프레소나 드립커피에 얼음을 추가하여 차게 만든 커피메뉴이다. 아이스커피는 핫(Hot) 커피메뉴와 마찬가지로 어떤 부재료를 사용하느냐에 따라 커피전문점별로 이름이 붙여지고 나라별로도 이름이 다르다.

**프라페**(프랑스어) Frappe
조각얼음을 넣어 차게 한 음료

**프레도**(이탈리아어) Freddo
거품이 있는 아이스음료. 셰이커에 에스프레소와 얼음, 찬물, 시럽을 넣고 셰이킹(Shaking)하여 찬 거품을 만든 것이다.

**샤커레토**(이탈리아어) Shakerrato
영어의 셰이커(Shaker)의 '흔들다'는 뜻. 셰이커에 얼음과 설탕, 에스프레소(Espresso)를 넣어 셰이킹(Shaking)하여 만든 메뉴.

**그라니타**(Granita)
과일, 설탕, 와인 등의 혼합물을 얼려 만든 얼음과자.

**셰이커**(Shaker)
셰이커는 재료를 담아 섞을 때 사용하는 용기이다. 커피를 차게 할 때 얼음과 함께 넣어 흔들어 커피만을 추출한다.

## Things to Be Considered When Ordering Coffee

### Coffee Size

Coffee shops may have different cup sizes. For instance, while one coffee shop has three sizes: short (240cc), tall (360cc), and grande (480cc), another coffee shop may have two sizes: small (240cc) and regular (360cc).

### Trendy Menus

Trendy menus are not available at all coffee shops. If you want to try one of them at a coffee shop, you need to check if the place has it. Check if the coffee shop you visit has them of you want to try one of them. Also, when you are not sure of some terms of coffee menus, it is recommended to confirm what they mean to the staff.

## 커피 주문 시에 참고할 사항

### 커피 사이즈(Coffee Size)

각 커피전문점에 따라 숏(Short 240cc), 톨(Tall 360cc), 그란데(Grande 480cc) 3가지 사이즈나 스몰(Small 240cc), 레귤러(Regular 360cc) 2가지 사이즈 등으로 분류한다.

### 유행커피

유행커피는 일부 매장에만 판매하고 취급하지 않는 매장도 있기에 주문할 때에는 이를 확인해야 한다. 그리고 커피메뉴 주문 시에 낯선 커피용어나 불확실한 메뉴는 매장직원에게 조언을 구하고 주문 하는 것이 좋다.

Latte
Mocha
Macchiato
Hot Chocolate
LOOSE LEAF TEAS
HOT DOGS
ICE CREAM
WAFFLES
SANDWICHES
CAKES

# 01
# Hand Drip

# 01. Hand Drip

## Straight Coffee
## 스트레이트 커피

This is a single-origin coffee brewed using a hand drip method (with a Kalita, Melitta, Kono, or Flannel dripper) rather than an espresso machine.

| | |
|---|---|
| Ingredients<br>재료 | • Whole beans with a single origin<br>• 단품 원두 |
| How to Make<br>만드는 방법 | • Brew 100 ml expresso from 15 gram whole beans with a single origin.<br>• Add hot water (90 to 95°C) to the pre-warmed cup.<br>• 단품 원두 15g을 핸드드립으로 100ml 추출한다.<br>• 예열된 잔에 따른 후 뜨거운 물(90~95℃) 70ml를 추가로 따른다. |

Type of glass

Santa tea cup
산타 티잔

Equipment
메뉴 만드는 기구

Drip sets (Kalita, Melitta, Flannel, or Hario)
드립 셋트(칼리타 · 멜리타 · 고노 · 융드립 · 하리오 등)

단품 원두로 에스프레소 머신이 아닌 핸드드립(칼리타, 멜리타, 고노, 융드립 등)으로 추출한 커피이다.

Follow the Steps
**▶▶| 추출 순서**

❶

❷

❸

❹

❺

❻

# 01. Hand Drip

## Aroma Melitta Brewing
## 아로마 멜리타 추출

Follow the Steps
▶▶| 추출 순서

❶
Grind whole beans.
원두 분쇄

❷
Prepare hot water at 90 to 95°C.
끓인 물 준비(90~95℃)

❸
Warm the cups.
잔 데우기

❹
Warm the dripper.
드립퍼 데우기

❺
Fold the filter.
필터 접기

❻
Place the filter inside the dripper.
필터 장착

❼
Put ground coffee.
분쇄커피 투입

❽
Soak the ground coffee.
뜸들이기(20~30초)

❾
Brew coffee.
커피 추출

❿
Serve the brewed coffee.
추출 완료

# 01. Hand Drip

## Flannel Drip
## 융드립

### Follow the Steps
### ▶▶| 추출 순서

❶
Soak the flannel filter.
융 적시기

❷
Remove water from the flannel filter.
융 물기 제거

❸
Warm the server.
서버 데우기

❹
Drain water from the server.
서버 물 비우기

❺
Pour water to infuse the ground coffee.
뜸들이는 물 붓기

❻
Infuse the ground coffee.
뜸들이기

❼
Brew the coffee.
커피 추출

❽
Coffee brewing is done.
커피 추출 완료

❾
Prepare a cup.
잔 준비

❿
Pour the brewed coffee to the cup.
커피 따르기

# 01. Hand Drip

## House Blend Coffee
## 하우스 블렌드 커피

This coffee is brewed from blended whole beans created and promoted by each coffee shop.

| | |
|---|---|
| **Ingredients**<br>재료 | • Santa or Rosa blend whole beans<br>• 산타 블렌딩 원두 혹은 로사 블렌딩 원두 |
| **How to Make**<br>만드는 방법 | • Prepare 15 grams of Santa or Rosa blend whole beans, and brew 100 ml of coffee by hand drip.<br>• Pour into the preheated cup, and add 70 ml hot water (90 to 95℃).<br>• 산타 블렌딩 원두 혹은 로사 블렌딩 원두15g을 핸드드립으로 100ml를 추출한다.<br>• 예열된 잔에 따른 후 뜨거운 물(90~95℃) 70ml를 추가로 따른다. |

Type of glass

Santa tea cup
산타 티잔

Equipment
메뉴 만드는 기구

Drip sets (Kalita, Melitta, Kono, Flannel, or Hario)
드립 셋트(칼리타, 멜리타, 고노, 융드립, 하리오 등)

커피전문점에서 자체적으로 블렌딩한 원두로 추출한 커피이다

Follow the Steps
▶▶| 추출 순서

❶

❷

❸

❹

❺

❻

## Dutch Coffee
## 더치커피

Dutch coffee is brewed by dropping water for about 12 hours at room temperature. This method gives coffee mature and neat flavors.

**Ingredients**
재료

- Dutch coffee concentrate and hot water
- 더치커피 원액, 뜨거운 물

**How to make**
만드는 방법

- Pour 50 ml of Dutch coffee concentrate to the pre-warmed cup.
- Add 200 ml of hot water to the cup.
- 예열된 잔에 더치커피 원액 50ml를 붓는다.
- 잔에 뜨거운 물 220ml를 추가로 따른다.

Type of glass

Santa mug
산타 머그잔

Equipment
메뉴 만드는 기구

Dutch coffee brewer
더치 추출기구

분쇄된 원두에 찬물을 12시간 정도 한방울씩 떨어뜨려 커피를 추출하는 방식으로, 숙성되고 깔끔한 향미를 느낄 수 있다.

Follow the Steps
▶▶| 만드는 순서

❶

❷

❸

❹

❺

❻

# 02
# Espresso

# 02. Espresso

## Espresso Single
## 에스프레소 싱글

Espresso is called the heart of coffee as it is the base of most coffee menus. Its strong, rich flavors linger in the mouth after tasting.

**Ingredients**
**재료**

- Whole beans for espresso
- 에스프레소용 원두

**How to Make**
**만드는 방법**

- Brew ground whole beans for espresso to a demitasse cup using a coffee machine. (7 ± 2 grams for 1 person / 16 grams for 2 persons)
  - If you are not familiar with espresso, you may want to add sugar. You will still be able to enjoy great flavors.
- 에스프레소용 원두를 사용하여 커피머신으로 데미타세(Demitasse) 잔에 에스프레소를 추출한다. (1인분 7 ± 2g, 2인분 16g)

※에스프레소를 처음 마실 경우에는 설탕을 넣어 마셔도 아주 좋은 향미를 즐길 수 있다.

Type of glass

Santa espresso cup
산타 에스프레소잔

Equipment
메뉴 만드는 기구

Espresso machine
에스프레소 머신

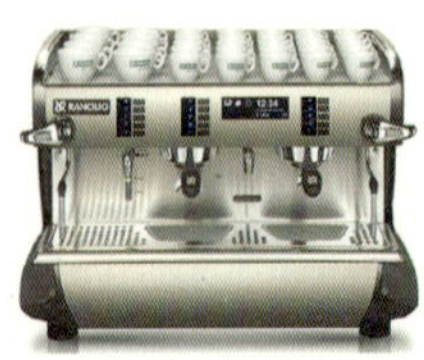

에스프레소는 커피의 심장이라고 말할 정도로 가장 기본이 되는 커피이다. 마시고 난 후 입안에 남는 커피의 진한 향미가 일품이다.

Follow the Steps
▶▶| 추출 순서

❶

❷

❸

❹

❺

❻

# 02. Espresso

## Espresso Double, Doppio
## 에스프레소 더블, 도피오

Doppio means "double" in Italian. You can enjoy double espressowith ease.

| Ingredients<br>재료 | • Whole beans for espresso<br>• 에스프레소용 원두 |
| --- | --- |
| How to Make<br>만드는 방법 | • Grind 16 grams of whole beans for espresso to make 2 shots of espresso. Brew the coffee to 1 doppio cup.<br>• 에스프레소용 원두 16g으로 커피머신에서 에스프레소 2샷을 도피오잔에 동시에 추출한다. |

Type of glass

Santa doppio cup
산타 도피오잔

Equipment
메뉴 만드는 기구

Espresso machine
에스프레소 머신

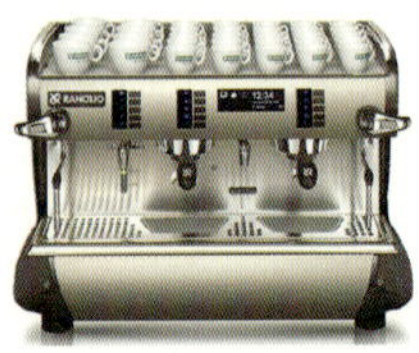

도피오는 이탈리아어로 '두 배'라는 뜻으로 에스프레소를 넉넉하게 즐길 수 있다.

Follow the Steps
▶▶| 추출 순서

❶

❷

❸

❹

❺

❻

## Americano
## 아메리카노

Americano is said to be an American-style brewed coffee, which is thin like drip coffee. Water is added to espresso to make it thinner.

| Ingredients 재료 | • Whole beans for espresso and hot water<br>• 에스프레소용 원두, 뜨거운 물 |
|---|---|
| How to Make 만드는 방법 | • Brew 1 shot of ground whole beans for espresso using a coffee machine.<br>• Pour 240 ml of hot water to the preheated mug, and add the brewed espresso.<br>• 에스프레소용 원두로 커피머신을 이용하여 스텐샷에 1샷을 추출한다.<br>• 예열된 머그잔에 뜨거운 물 240ml를 받은 후 에스프레소 1샷을 따른다. |

Type of glass

Santa mug
산타 머그잔

Equipment
메뉴 만드는 기구

Espresso machine
에스프레소 머신

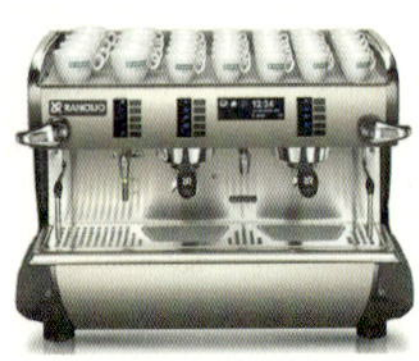

미국에서는 드립방식의 연한 커피를 의미하며 일반적으로는 에스프레소에 물을 부어 연하게 마시는 커피를 뜻한다.

Follow the Steps

**▶▶| 만드는 순서**

❶

❷

❸

❹

❺

❻

## Rosa Double Espresso
## 로사 더블 에스프레소

This is an attractive coffee menu with balanced flavors of ristretto and Irish whiskey, sweet caramel, savory vanilla, and soft whipped cream.

### Ingredients
재료

- Whole beans for espresso, vanilla syrup, Irish syrup, whipped cream, and caramel sauce
- 에스프레소용 원두, 바닐라 시럽, 아이리쉬 크림시럽, 휘핑크림, 캐러멜 소스

### How to Make
만드는 방법

- Put ½ pumps of vanilla syrup and 5 drops of Irish cream syrups into a doppio cup.
- Using ground whole beans for espresso, brew 2 shots of ristretto to a cup.
- Fill the cup up to 90% with steamed milk.
- Add whipped cream on the top of it, and decorate with caramel sauce.

- 도피오잔에 바닐라시럽(1/2 펌핑)과 아이리쉬 크림시럽(5방울)을 넣는다.
- 에스프레소용 원두로 리스트레또 2샷을 준비된 잔에 추출한다.
- 스팀우유를 잔의 90%까지 따른다.
- 휘핑크림을 올린 후 캐러멜소스로 토핑을 한다.

Type of glass

Santa doppio cup
산타 도피오잔

Equipment
메뉴 만드는 기구

Espresso machine & cream whipper
에스프레소 머신 · 휘핑기

진한 리스트레토와 아이리쉬 위스키, 캐러멜, 바닐라의 향미에 부드러운 생크림이 어우러진 매력적인 커피 메뉴이다.

Follow the Steps
▶▶| 만드는 순서

❶

❷

❸

❹

❺

❻

# Espresso Con Panna
# 에스프레소 콘파나

"Con panna" is a compound word combining "con" meaning "to mix" and "panna" which meaning "cream" in Italian. Thus, con panna refers to espresso coffee topped with cream.

| Ingredients<br>재료 | • Whole beans for espresso and whipped cream<br>• 에스프레소용 원두, 휘핑크림 |
|---|---|
| How to Make<br>만드는 방법 | • Brew ground whole beans for espresso to a demitasse cup using a coffee machine.<br>• Add some of whipped cream on top.<br>• 에스프레소용 원두로 커피머신을 이용하여 데미타세 잔에 에스프레소를 추출한다.<br>• 휘핑크림을 올린다. |

Type of glass

Santa espresso cup
산타 에스프레소잔

Equipment
메뉴 만드는 기구

Espresso machine & cream whipper
에스프레소 머신 · 휘핑기

콘파냐 (Con Panna)는 이탈리아어로 Con(혼합, 섞다)과 Panna(생크림)의 합성어로 에스프레소에 생크림을 올린 커피이다.

Follow the Steps
▶▶| 만드는 순서

❶

❷

❸

❹

❺

❻

# 02. Espresso

## Espresso Macchiato
## 에스프레소 마끼아또

Macchiatt means "marked" or "stained" in Italian. Traditionally, macchiato was a shot of espresso with just a small amount of steamed milk foam which looked like "stains" on the expresso.

**Ingredients**
**재료**

- Whole beans for espresso and steamed milk
- 에스프레소용 원두, 스팀우유

**How to Make**
**만드는 방법**

- Brew ground whole beans for espresso to a demitasse cup using a coffee machine.
- Add 1 spoon of steamed milk foam on top.
- For a finishing touch, pour steamed milk in the middle of the demitasse cup.

- 에스프레소용 원두로 커피머신을 이용하여 데미타세 잔에 에스프레소를 추출한다.
- 스티밍된 우유거품을 한 스푼 떠서 올린다.
- 스팀우유를 데미타세 잔 중앙에 부어서 마무리 한다.

Type of glass

Santa espresso cup
산타 에스프레소잔

Equipment
메뉴 만드는 기구

Espresso machine, steam pitcher & milk spoon
에스프레소 머신 · 스팀피처 · 우유스푼

마끼아또 (Macchiato)는 이탈리아어로 '얼룩지다'라는 뜻이며 본래는 에스프레소에 얼룩질 정도의 소량의 우유거품을 넣어 마시는 것에서 유래하였다.

Follow the Steps
▶▶I 만드는 순서

❶

❷

❸

❹

❺

❻

03

# Cafè Latte & Cappuccino

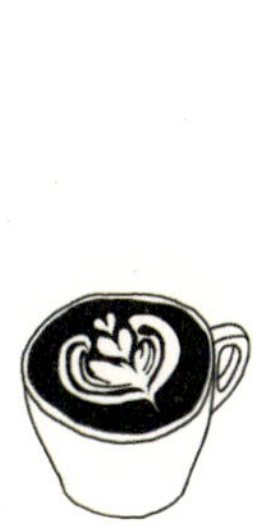

# 03. Caffè Latte & Cappuccino

## Caffè Latte
카페라떼

This is one of the most iconic coffees. It combines milk and coffee. Milk gives espresso a soft flavor and texture.

| | |
|---|---|
| Ingredients<br>재료 | • Whole beans for espresso and steamed milk<br>• 에스프레소용 원두, 스팀우유 |
| How to Make<br>만드는 방법 | Use a Santa tea cup<br>• Brew 1 shot of espresso to a tea cup.<br>• Create your own latte art by pouring steamed milk to the tea cup.<br>산타 티잔 사용<br>• 티잔에 에스프레소 1샷을 추출한다.<br>• 스팀우유를 이용하여 티잔에 따르면서 아트를 그린다. |

Type of glass

Santa tea cup
산타 티잔

Equipment
메뉴 만드는 기구

Espresso machine & steam pitcher
에스프레소 머신 · 스팀피처

에스프레소에 우유를 넣어 부드럽게 마시는 '우유+커피'의 대명사이다.

Follow the Steps
▶▶I 만드는 순서

❶

❷

❸

❹

❺

❻

# 03. Caffè Latte & Cappuccino

## How to Make
만드는 방법

**Use a Santa latte cup**
- Brew 2 shots of ristretto to a latte cup.
- Create your own latte art by pouring steamed milk to the latte cup.

**산타 라떼잔 사용**
- 라떼잔에 리스트레또 2샷을 추출한다.
- 스팀우유를 이용하여 라떼잔에 따르면서 아트를 그린다.

Type of glass

Santa latte cup
산타 라떼잔

Follow the Steps

▶▶| 만드는 순서

❶

❷

❸

❹

❺

❻

# 03. Caffè Latte & Cappuccino

## Vanilla Caffè Latte
## 바닐라 카페라떼

This coffee presents a good balance of rich espresso, warm milk, and sweet vanilla flavors

**Ingredients**
재료

- Whole beans for espresso, vanilla syrup, and steamed milk
- 에스프레소용 원두, 바닐라시럽, 스팀우유

**How to Make**
만드는 방법

Use a Santa tea cup

- Put ½ pumps of vanilla syrup to a tea cup.
- Brew 1 shot of espresso to the tea cup with vanilla syrup.
- Create your own latte art pouring steamed milk to the tea cup.

산타 티잔 사용

- 티잔에 바닐라시럽 1/2 펌핑을 한다.
- 바닐라시럽을 넣은 티잔에 에스프레소 1샷을 추출한다.
- 스팀우유를 이용하여 티잔에 따르면서 아트를 그린다.

Type of glass

Santa tea cup
산타 티잔

Equipment
메뉴 만드는 기구

Espresso machine & steam pitcher
에스프레소 머신 · 스팀피처

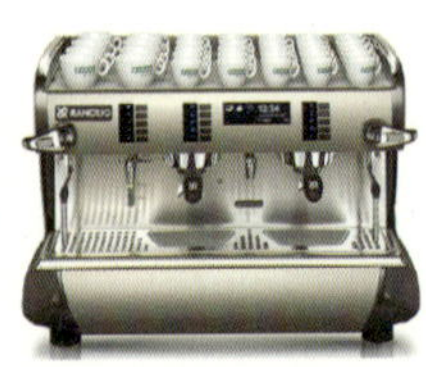

에스프레소와 따뜻한 우유 그리고 부드러운 바닐라 향이 어우러진 커피이다.

Follow the Steps
▶▶| 만드는 순서

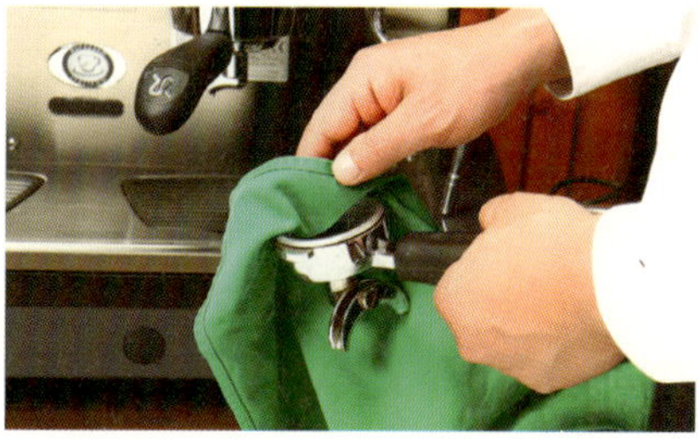

❶

❷

❸

❹

❺

❻

# 03. Caffè Latte & Cappuccino

## How to Make
만드는 방법

### Use a Latte tea cup

- Put 1 pump of vanilla syrup to a latte cup.
- Brew 2 shots of ristretto to the latte cup with vanilla syrup.
- Create your own latte art by pouring steamed milk to the latte cup.

### 산타 라떼잔 사용

- 라떼잔에 바닐라시럽 1펌핑을 한다.
- 바닐라시럽을 넣은 라떼잔에 리스트레또 2샷을 추출한다.
- 스팀우유를 이용하여 라떼잔에 따르면서 아트를 그린다.

Type of glass

Santa latte cup
산타 라떼잔

Follow the Steps
▶▶| 만드는 순서

❶

❷

❸

❹

❺

❻

# 03. Caffè Latte & Cappuccino

## Caramel Caffè Latte
## 캐러멜 카페라떼

This coffee is beloved for its balance of soft milk and sweet caramel flavors.

**Ingredients**
재료

- Whole beans for espresso, caramel syrup, and steamed milk
- 에스프레소용 원두, 캐러멜시럽, 스팀우유

**How to Make**
만드는 방법

Use a Santa tea cup
- Put ½ pumps of vanilla syrup to a tea cup.
- Brew 1 shot of espresso to the tea cup with vanilla syrup.
- Create your own latte art by pouring steamed milk to the tea cup.

산타 티잔 사용
- 티잔에 캐러멜시럽 1/2 펌핑을 한다.
- 캐러멜시럽을 넣은 티잔에 에스프레소 1샷을 추출한다.
- 스팀우유를 이용하여 티잔에 따르면서 아트를 그린다.

Type of glass

Santa tea cup
산타 티잔

Equipment
메뉴 만드는 기구

Espresso machine & steam pitcher
에스프레소 머신 · 스팀피처

커피와 부드러운 우유에 달콤한 캐러멜 향이 매력적인 커피이다.

Follow the Steps

▶▶| 만드는 순서

❶

❷

❸

❹

❺

❻

# 03. Caffè Latte & Cappuccino

## How to Make
만드는 방법

### Use a Santa latte cup

- Put ½ pumps of vanilla syrup to a latte cup.
- Brew 2 shots of ristretto to the latte cup with vanilla syrup.
- Create your own latte art by pouring steamed milk to the latte cup.

### 산타 라떼잔 사용

- 라떼잔에 캐러멜시럽 1펌핑을 한다.
- 캐러멜시럽을 넣은 라떼잔에 리스트레또 2샷을 추출한다.
- 스팀우유를 이용하여 라떼잔에 따르면서 아트를 그린다.

Type of glass

Santa latte cup
산타 라떼잔

Follow the Steps
▶▶| 만드는 순서

❶

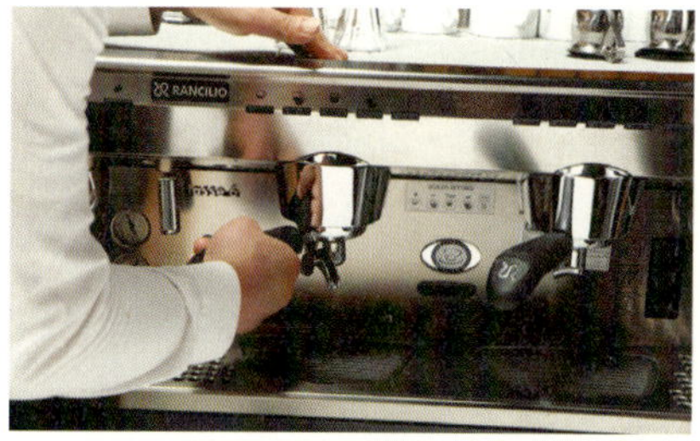


❷

❸

❹

❺

❻

# 03. Caffè Latte & Cappuccino

## Cappuccino
## 카푸치노

This menu is espresso with milk foam on top. You can enjoy the soft texture of milk foam while sipping coffee.

| | |
|---|---|
| Ingredients<br>재료 | • Whole beans for espresso, steamed milk, and cinnamon powder<br>• 에스프레소용 원두, 스팀우유, 시나몬 파우더 |

**How to Make**
만드는 방법

**Cappuccino Scuro**
- Brew 1 shot of espresso to a cappuccino cup.
- Put 3 to 4 spoons of milk foam on top, and pour steamed milk to fill up the cappuccino cup.
- Use cinnamon powder as a topping.

**카푸치노 스쿠로**
- 카푸치노잔에 에스프레소 1샷을 추출한다.
- 우유거품을 3~4회 스푼으로 떠 올린 후 스팀우유를 부어 카푸치노잔을 채운다.
- 시나몬 파우더로 토핑을 한다.

Type of glass

Santa cappuccinp cup
산타 카푸치노잔

Equipment
메뉴 만드는 기구
Espresso machine, steam pitcher, milk spoon & cappuccino decorator
에스프레소 머신 · 스팀피처 · 우유스푼 · 카푸치노 데코레이터 에스프레소에 우유거품을 얹어 마시는 메뉴로 커피를 마시면서 닿는 부드러운 우유 거품의 조화가 매력적이다.

Follow the Steps
▶▶| 만드는 순서

❶

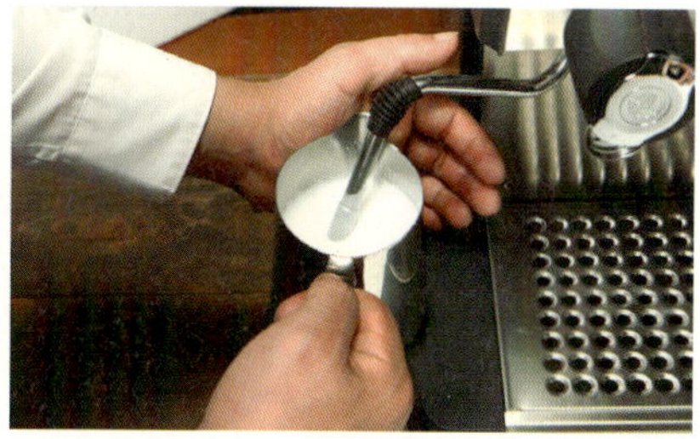

❷

❸

❹

❺

❻

# 03. Caffè Latte & Cappuccino

## How to Make
만드는 방법

**Cappuccino Chiaro**
- Brew 1 shot of espresso to a cappuccino cup.
- Sprinkle cinnamon powder on the brewed coffee.
- Fill the cappuccino cup with steamed milk.

**카푸치노 치아로**
- 카푸치노잔에 에스프레소 1샷을 추출한다.
- 추출된 잔에 시나몬 파우더를 뿌려준다.
- 스팀우유를 부어 카푸치노잔을 채운다.

Type of glass

Santa cappuccinp cup
산타 카푸치노잔

Follow the Steps
▶▶| 만드는 순서

❶

❷

❸

❹

❺

❻

# 04
# Variations

## Caffè Vienna
## 카페 비엔나

Originating from Einspänner of Vienna, Austria, this coffee has a graceful presentation with whipped cream added on top.

### Ingredients
재료

- Rosa blend whole beans, sugar syrup, and whipped cream
- 로사 블렌딩 원두, 설탕시럽, 휘핑크림

### How to Make
만드는 방법

Caffè vienna brewed using a flannel drip method
- Put ½ sugar syrup pumps to a tea cup.
- Grind 25 grams of Rosa blend whole beans. Brew the ground coffee to brew 150 ml coffee to the tea cup.
- Add whipped cream on top.

융드립 카페 비엔나
- 티잔에 설탕시럽 1/2펌핑을 한다.
- 로사 블렌딩 원두 25g으로 융드립하여 150ml를 추출하여 티잔에 따른다.
- 휘핑크림을 올린다.

Type of glass

Santa tea cup
산타 티잔

Equipment
메뉴 만드는 기구

Flannel drip set & cream whipper
융드립 셋트 · 휘핑기

오스트리아 비엔나의 아인슈패너에서 유래된 커피로 휘핑 크림을 올린 고풍스러운 메뉴이다.

Follow the Steps
▶▶| 만드는 순서

❶

❷

❸

❹

❺

❻

# 04. Variations

## How to Make
만드는 방법

### Espresso Caffè vienna

- Put ½ sugar syrup pumps in a tea cup.
- Pour 130 ml of hot water in the tea cup.
- Brew 1 shot of espresso, and add it to the tea cup.
- Add whipped cream on top.

### 에스프레소 카페 비엔나

- 티잔에 설탕시럽 1/2펌핑을 한다.
- 티잔에 뜨거운 물 130ml를 받는다.
- 에스프레소 1샷을 추출하여 티잔에 따른다.
- 휘핑크림을 올린다.

Type of glass

Santa tea cup
산타 티잔

Equipment
메뉴 만드는 기구

Espresso machine & cream whipper
에스프레소 머신 · 휘핑기

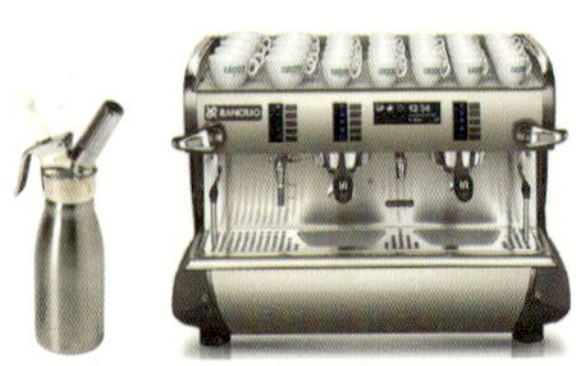

Follow the Steps
▶▶| 만드는 순서

❶

❷

❸

❹

❺

❻

## Caffè Mocha-Java
## 카페 모카자바

When chocolate syrup or sauce is added to a coffee menu, it will usually have the word 'Mocha' in its name. Chocolate sauce and whipped cream on top gives the coffee, which was brewed using a flannel dripper, a lingering fragrance and sweetness in the mouth.

### Ingredients
재료

- Rosa blend whole beans, chocolate sauce, whipped cream, and chocolate powder

- 로사 블렌딩 원두, 초코소스, 휘핑크림, 초코 파우더

### How to Make
만드는 방법

- Put ½ chocolate sauce pumps to a tea cup.
- Grind 25 grams of Rosa blend whole beans. Using a flannel dripper, brew 150 ml coffee to the tea cup.
- Mix the coffee and chocolate sauce well in the tea cup.
- Add whipped cream on top and sprinkle chocolate powder.

- 티잔에 초코소스 1/2펌핑을 한다.
- 로사 블렌딩 원두 25g을 융드립 서버 기준으로 150ml를 추출하여 티잔에 따른다.
- 티잔의 커피와 초코소스가 혼합이 되도록 섞는다.
- 휘핑크림을 올린 후 초코소스와 초코파우더로 토핑을 한다.

Type of glass

Santa tea cup
산타 티잔

Equipment
메뉴 만드는 기구

Flannel drip set & cream whipper
융드립 셋트 · 휘핑기

보통 커피메뉴에서는 초콜릿 시럽이나 소스가 첨가된 경우 '모카'라는 단어가 들어간다. 이 메뉴는 융드립한 커피에 초코소스와 생크림이 올라가 향기로우면서도 달콤한 여운을 남겨준다.

Follow the Steps
▶▶| 만드는 순서

❶

❷

❸

❹

❺

❻

# 04. Variations

## Caffè Mocha
## 카페모카

Milk, chocolate sauce, and whipped cream give espresso the rich and sweet touch of chocolate.

**Ingredients**
재료

- Whole beans for espresso, chocolate sauce, steamed milk, whipped cream, and chocolate powder
- 에스프레소용 원두, 초코소스, 스팀우유, 휘핑크림, 초코파우더

**How to Make**
만드는 방법

- Put 1 chocolate sauce pump to a mug.
- Brew 2 shots of ristretto, and mix it well with chocolate sauce.
- Pour steam milk up to 90% of the mug.
- Add whipped cream on top, and decorate with chocolate sauce and chocolate powder.

- 머그잔에 초코소스 1펌핑을 한다.
- 리스트레또 2샷을 추출하여 초코소스와 혼합한다.
- 스팀우유를 잔의 90%까지 붓는다.
- 휘핑크림을 올린 후 초코소스와 초코파우더로 토핑을 한다.

Type of glass

Santa mug
산타 머그잔

Equipment
메뉴 만드는 기구

Espresso machine
steam pitcher & cream whipper
에스프레소 머신 · 스팀피처 · 휘핑기

에스프레소에 우유와 초코소스, 생크림이 올라가 진한 초콜릿의 달콤함이 느껴지는 커피 메뉴이다.

Follow the Steps
▶▶I 만드는 순서

❶

❷

❸

❹

❺

❻

# 04. Variations

## Caramel Macchiato
## 캐러멜 마끼아또

This menu presents a pleasant harmony between the fragrant caramel syrup, the rich flavor of espresso, and soft milk foam. The sweet savory caramel syrup makes it as one of the most popular coffees.

### Ingredients
재료

- Whole beans for espresso, caramel syrup, steamed milk, and caramel sauce
- 에스프레소용 원두, 캐러멜시럽, 스팀우유, 캐러멜소스

### How to Make
만드는 방법

- Put 1 caramel syrup pump to a mug.
- Extract 2 shots of ristretto to the mug.
- Pour steamed milk.
- Drizzle caramel sauce on top.

- 머그잔에 캐러멜시럽 1펌핑을 한다.
- 머그잔에 리스트레또 2샷을 추출한다.
- 스팀우유를 붓는다.
- 캐러멜소스로 토핑을 한다.

Type of glass

Santa mug
산타 머그잔

Equipment
메뉴 만드는 기구

Espresso machine & steam pitcher
에스프레소 머신 · 스팀피처

향긋한 캐러멜 시럽이 에스프레소의 진한 맛에 부드러운 우유거품과 함께 조화를 이룬 커피 메뉴이다. 캐러멜의 달콤한 맛이 감미로워 대중적으로 선호하는 커피메뉴 중 하나이다.

Follow the Steps
▶▶| 만드는 순서

❶

❷

❸

❹

❺

❻

## Café Royale
## 카페 로얄

It is said that Napoleon enjoyed "café royale." Brandy, a heavy alcohol, results in a fancy presentation with a blue flame.

### Ingredients
### 재료

- Rosa blend whole beans, Irish cream syrup, lump sugar, and brandy
- 로사 블렌딩 원두, 아이리쉬 크림시럽, 각설탕, 브랜디

### How to Make
### 만드는 방법

- Put 5 cream syrup drops to a tea cup.
- Grind 25 grams of Rosa blend whole beans. Brew 150 ml coffee to the tea cup.
- Rest a royal spoon over the cup, and put a sugar cube on the spoon.
- Let the sugar cube soaked with brandy. Set a flame on it.

- 티잔에 아이리쉬 크림시럽 5방울을 넣는다.
- 로사블렌딩 원두 25g을 융드립으로 서버기준 150ml를 추출하여 티잔에 따른다.
- 로얄스푼을 잔에 걸고 각설탕을 올린다
- 각설탕에 브랜디를 적신 후 불을 붙인다.

Type of glass

Santa tea cup
산타 티잔

Equipment
메뉴 만드는 기구

Flannel drip set & royal coffee spoon
융드립 셋트 · 로얄커피스푼

'왕족의 커피'라는 의미의 카페 로얄은 나폴레옹이 자주 마셨다는 칵테일이다. 알코올 도수가 높은 브랜디의 푸른 불빛이 특별한 분위기를 연출한다.

Follow the Steps
▶▶| 만드는 순서

❶

❷

❸

❹

❺

❻

## Café au Lait
카페오레

Au lait' means 'with milk' in French. Brew coffee using flannel drip, and then add steamed milk

**Ingredients**
재료

- Rosa blend whole beans and steamed milk
- 로사 블렌딩 원두, 스팀우유

**How to Make**
만드는 방법

- Brew 20 grams of Rosa blend whole beans to brew 100 ml coffee using a flannel drip.
- Pour it to the cup.
- Add 70 ml of water to the tea cup.

- 로사 블렌딩 원두 20g으로 융드립하여 100ml를 추출한다.
- 티잔에 따른다.
- 스팀우유 70ml을 추가로 티잔에 따른다.

Type of glass

Santa tea cup
산타 티잔

Equipment
메뉴 만드는 기구

Flannel drip set, espresso machine & steam pitcher
융드립 셋트 · 에스프레소 머신 · 스팀피처

'오레'는 프랑스어로 '우유가 들어간'을 뜻하며
원두를 융드립으로 추출한 후 스팀우유를 더한 커피이다.

Follow the Steps
▶▶| 만드는 순서

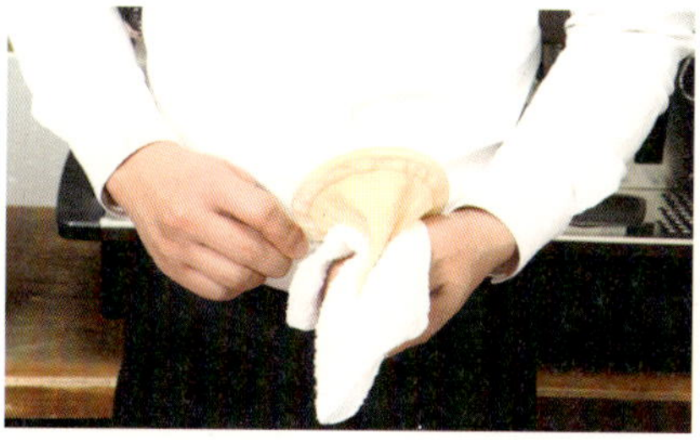
❶

❷

❸

❹

❺

❻

## Santa Café Cocoa
## 산타 카페 코코아

Mexican spice and cocoa add rich flavors to this sweet espresso.

**Ingredients**
재료

- Whole beans for espresso, Mexican spice cocoa powder, cinnamon powder, and steamed milk
- 에스프레소용 원두, 멕시칸 스파이스 코코아파우더, 시나몬 파우더, 스팀우유

**How to Make**
만드는 방법

- Put 32 grams of Mexican spice cocoa powder and cinnamon powder a little in a mug.
- Brew 2 cups of ristretto to the mug, and mix it well.
- Pour the steamed milk.

- 머그잔에 멕시칸 스파이스 코코아파우더 32g과 시나몬파우더 소량을 넣는다.
- 리스트레또 2샷을 머그잔에 추출한 후 혼합한다.
- 스팀우유를 따른다.

Type of glass

Santa mug
산타 머그잔

Equipment
메뉴 만드는 기구

Espresso machine & steam pitcher
에스프레소 머신 · 스팀피처

멕시칸 스파이스 코코아를 이용한 메뉴로 에스프레소와 멕시칸 스파이스, 초콜릿 등이 어우러져 풍성한 느낌을 주는 달콤한 음료이다.

Follow the Steps
▶▶| 만드는 순서

❶

❷

❸

❹

❺

❻

# 05
# Iced Coffee Menus

# 05. Iced Coffee Menus

## Iced House Blend Coffee
## 아이스 하우스 커피

This iced coffee is made by brewing whole beans blended by Santarosa. A Melitta Aroma dripper is used.

| Ingredients<br>재료 | • Santa or Rosa blend whole beans and ice<br>• 산타 블렌딩 원두, 얼음 |
|---|---|
| How to Make<br>만드는 방법 | • Put 7 to 8 ice cubes. Brew 15 grams of Santa or Rosa blend whole beans to make 250 ml coffee using the Aroma Melitta hand drip.<br>• Put 6 ice cubes in an ice glass.<br>• Pour brewed coffee to the ice glass.<br>• 서버에 얼음을 7~8개 넣고, 산타 블렌딩 원두 혹은 로사 블렌딩 원두 15g을 아로마 멜리타로 핸드드립을 하여 서버 기준으로 250ml를 추출한다.<br>• 아이스잔에 얼음 6개를 담는다.<br>• 추출된 커피를 아이스잔에 따른다. |

Type of glass

Wine glass
와인 잔

Equipment
메뉴 만드는 기구

Aroma Melitta drip set
아로마 멜리타 드립 셋트

산타로사에서 블렌딩한 커피원두를 아로마 멜리타드립으로 추출한 아이스커피이다.

Follow the Steps

▶▶| 만드는 순서

❶

❷

❸

❹

❺

❻

# 05. Iced Coffee Menus

## Iced Dutch Coffee
## 아이스 더치커피

Iced Dutch coffee had neat tastes compared to iced americano.

**Ingredients**
재료

- Dutch coffee concentrate, cold water, ice, and syrup
- 더치커피 원액, 차가운 물, 얼음, 시럽

**How to Make**
만드는 방법

- Fill the ice glass up 70% of it.
- Pour 100 ml of Dutch coffee concentrate to the ice glass.
  - You may want to add sugar syrup according to your preference.
- Fill the glass up to 80% with cold water.
- Stir it until Dutch coffee concentrate and water are mixed well.
- Fill the ice glass with extra ice.

- 아이스잔에 얼음을 70% 정도 채운다.
- 더치원액 100ml를 아이스잔에 따른다.
  ※기호에 따라 설탕시럽을 추가해도 좋다.
- 차가운 물을 잔의 80% 정도까지 채운다.
- 더치커피 원액과 물이 잘 섞이도록 저어준다.
- 추가로 얼음을 아이스잔에 가득 채운다.

Type of glass

Santa ice glass
산타 아이스잔

Equipment
메뉴 만드는 기구

Dutch coffee brewer
더치추출기구

아이스 더치커피는 일반적인 아이스 아메리카노와는 달리 깔끔한 맛이 장점이다.

Follow the Steps
▶▶| 만드는 순서

❶

❷

❸

❹

❺

❻

# 05. Iced Coffee Menus

## Iced Americano
## 아이스 아메리카노

This menu is simply enjoyed by adding espresso to iced water. It is an easy and refreshing beverage for the summer.

**Ingredients**
재료

- Whole beans for espresso, cold water, and ice
- 에스프레소용 원두, 차가운 물, 얼음

**How to Make**
만드는 방법

- Fill an ice glass with ice.
- Pour cold water up to 80% of the glass.
- Brew 2 shots of espresso. Pour the brewed espresso to the ice glass.

- 아이스잔에 얼음을 가득 채운다.
- 찬물을 잔의 80%까지 채운다.
- 에스프레소 2샷을 추출하여 아이스잔에 붓는다.

Type of glass

Santa ice glass
산타 아이스잔

Equipment
메뉴 만드는 기구

Espresso machine
에스프레소 머신

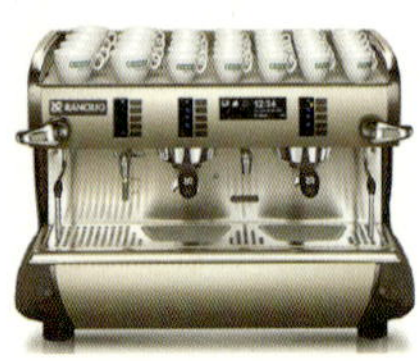

얼음물에 에스프레소를 넣은 커피로 더운 여름에 시원하고 간편하게 즐길 수 있다.

Follow the Steps
▶▶| 만드는 순서

❶

❷

❸

❹

❺

❻

# 05. Iced Coffee Menus

## Café Freddo
## 카페 프레도

This menu includes a shaking step that mixes americano and ice. It has softer and richer flavors than iced americano.

**Ingredients**
재료

- Whole beans for espresso, cold water, and ice
- 에스프레소용 원두, 차가운 물, 얼음

**How to Make**
만드는 방법

Iced coffee made with a shaker

- Put 6 ice cubes, 100 ml of cold water, and 2 shots of espresso in the shaker. Shake them all together.
- Fill the half of the ice glass with ice.
- Pour the coffee in the shaker to the ice glass.

**Shaker를 사용한 아이스커피**

- 셰이커에 얼음( 6개)과 냉수(100ml)를 준비한 뒤 에스프레소 2샷을 추출하여 함께 넣고 셰이킹을 한다.
- 아이스잔에 얼음 절반을 채운다.
- 준비된 아이스잔에 셰이킹한 커피를 붓는다.

Type of glass

Santa ice glass
산타 아이스잔

Equipment
메뉴 만드는 기구

Espresso machine & shaker
에스프레소 머신 · 셰이커

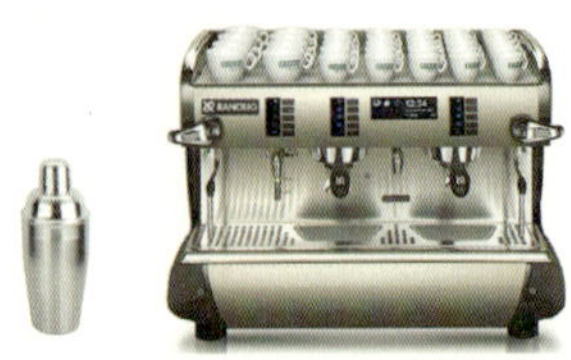

아메리카노와 얼음을 셰이킹하여 마시는 커피로
아이스 아메리카노에 비해 부드럽고 풍성한 향이 특징이다.

Follow the Steps
**만드는 순서**

❶

❷

❸

❹

❺

❻

# 05. Iced Coffee Menus

## Iced Café Latte
## 아이스 카페라떼

This iced coffee menu has a soft flavor and texture, which is a result of the milk foam topped on the mixture of espresso, ice, and milk.

| | |
|---|---|
| Ingredients<br>재료 | • Whole beans for espresso, milk, and ice<br>• 에스프레소용 원두, 우유, 얼음 |
| How to Make<br>만드는 방법 | • Fill the ice glass with ice.<br>• Pour milk up to 80% of the glass.<br>• Brew 2 shots of espresso, and pour it to the glass.<br>• Add milk foam on top.<br>• 아이스잔에 얼음을 가득 채운다.<br>• 잔의 80%까지 우유를 따른다.<br>• 에스프레소 2샷을 추출하여 아이스잔에 붓는다.<br>• 우유거품을 얹는다. |

Type of glass

Santa ice glass
산타 아이스잔

Equipment
메뉴 만드는 기구

Espresso machine, foam maker & milk spoon
에스프레소 머신 · 거품기 · 우유스푼

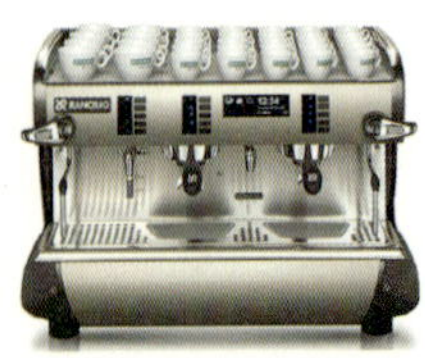

얼음에 우유와 에스프레소를 넣은 뒤 우유거품을 살짝 얹어 마시는 부드러운 아이스 커피 메뉴이다.

Follow the Steps
▶▶I 만드는 순서

❶

❷

❸

❹

❺

❻

# 05. Iced Coffee Menus

## Iced Vanilla Café Latte
## 아이스 바닐라 카페라떼

This menu presents a fragrant vanilla flavor over coffee, ice, and milk.

**Ingredients**
**재료**

- Whole beans for espresso, vanilla syrup, milk, and ice
- 에스프레소용 원두, 바닐라시럽, 우유, 얼음

**How to Make**
**만드는 방법**

- Fill the ice glass with ice.
- Put 2 vanilla syrup pumps to the glass.
  Pour milk up to 80% of the glass.
- Brew 2 shots of espresso, and pour it to the glass.
- Add milk foam on top.

- 아이스잔에 얼음을 가득 채운다.
- 아이스잔에 바닐라시럽 2펌핑을 하고, 우유를 잔의 80%까지 붓는다.
- 에스프레소 2샷을 추출하여 붓는다.
- 우유거품을 얹는다.

Type of glass

Santa ice glass
산타 아이스잔

Equipment
메뉴 만드는 기구

Espresso machine, foam maker & milk spoon
에스프레소 머신 · 거품기 · 우유스푼

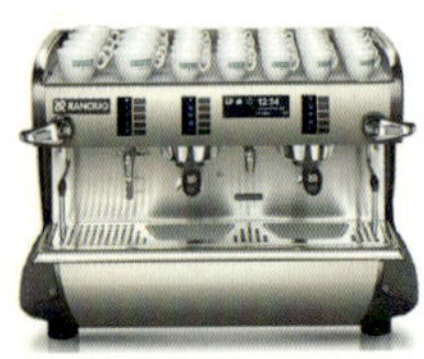

얼음에 커피와 우유가 어우러진 향긋한 바닐라향의 커피이다.

Follow the Steps
▶▶| 만드는 순서

❶

❷

❸

❹

❺

❻

# 05. Iced Coffee Menus

## Iced Caramel Café Latte
## 아이스 캐러멜 카페라떼

**Ingredients**
재료

- Whole beans for espresso, caramel syrup, milk, and ice
- 에스프레소용 원두, 캐러멜시럽, 우유, 얼음

**How to Make**
만드는 방법

- Fill the ice glass with ice.
- Put 2 caramel syrup pumps to the glass. Pour milk up to 80% of the glass.
- Brew 2 shots of espresso, and pour it to the glass.
- Add milk foam on top.

- 아이스잔에 얼음을 가득 채운다.
- 아이스잔에 캐러멜시럽 2펌핑을 하고, 우유를 잔의 80%까지 따른다.
- 에스프레소 2샷을 추출하여 붓는다.
- 우유거품을 얹는다.

Type of glass

Santa ice glass
산타 아이스잔

Equipment
메뉴 만드는 기구

Espresso machine, foam maker & milk spoon
에스프레소 머신 · 거품기 · 우유스푼

캐러멜 카페라떼를 시원하게 마시는 메뉴로서 카페라떼와는 다른 달콤함을 선사한다.

Follow the Steps
▶▶I 만드는 순서

❶

❷

❸

❹

❺

❻

# 05. Iced Coffee Menus

## Iced Cappuccino
## 아이스 카푸치노

**Ingredients**
재료

- Whole beans for espresso, milk, ice, and cinnamon powder
- 에스프레소용 원두, 우유, 얼음, 시나몬파우더

**How to Make**
만드는 방법

**Making iced cappuccino**
- Fill the ice glass with ice.
- Pour milk up to 60% of the glass.
- Brew 2 shots of espresso, and pour it to the glass.
- Add cinnamon power as a topping.

**아이스 카푸치노 빌딩**
- 아이스잔에 얼음을 가득 채운다.
- 잔의 60%까지 우유를 따른다.
- 에스프레소 2샷을 추출하여 아이스잔에 따른다.
- 우유거품을 얹는다.
- 시나몬파우더로 토핑을 한다.

Type of glass

Santa ice glass
산타 아이스잔

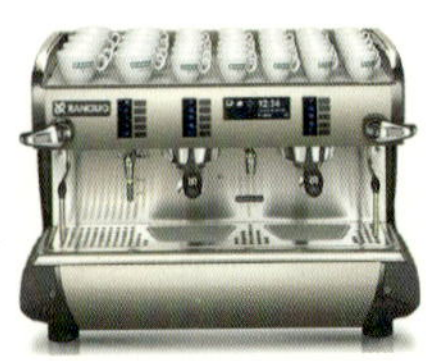

Equipment
메뉴 만드는 기구

Espresso machine, foam maker & milk spoon
에스프레소 머신 · 거품기 · 우유스푼

풍성한 우유거품과 진한 에스프레소가 부드럽게 어우러진 아이스 커피 메뉴이다.

Follow the Steps
▶▶I 만드는 순서

❶

❷

❸

❹

❺

❻

# 05. Iced Coffee Menus

## How to Make
만드는 방법

### Cappuccion Shaking
- Put 12 to 13 ice cubes and 125 ml of milk in the shaker.
- Brew 2 shots of espresso. Pour the espresso into the shaker. Shake it to mix the ingredients.
- Pour the mixture to the ice glass.
- Add milk foam on top.
- Sprinkle cinnamon powder.

### 카푸치노 셰이킹
- 셰이커에 얼음 12~13개를 넣고, 우유 125ml를 붓는다.
- 에스프레소 2샷을 추출하여 셰이커에 붓고 셰이킹을 한다.
- 셰이킹된 것을 아이스잔에 따른다.
- 우유거품을 얹는다.
- 시나몬파우더로 토핑을 한다.

Type of glass

Santa ice glass
산타 아이스잔

Follow the Steps
▶▶| 만드는 순서

❶

❷

❸

❹

❺

❻

# 05. Iced Coffee Menus

## Iced Café Mocha
## 아이스 카페모카

This is the cold menu of café mocha, with a subtle balance between sweet and bitter tastes.

### Ingredients
### 재료

- Whole beans for espresso, chocolate sauce, milk, ice, whipped cream, and chocolate powder
- 에스프레소용 원두, 초코소스, 우유, 얼음, 휘핑크림, 초코파우더

### How to Make
### 만드는 방법

- Put 2 chocolate sauce pumps to the ice glass.
- Brew 2 shots of espresso, and mix it with chocolate sauce.
- Fill the ice glass with ice. Pour milk up to 70% of the glass.
- Add a little milk foam on top. Add whipped cream again.
- Add chocolate powder and chocolate sauce as toppings.

- 아이스잔에 초코소스 2펌핑을 한다.
- 에스프레소 2샷을 추출하여 초코소스와 혼합을 한다.
- 아이스잔에 얼음을 채운 후 우유를 잔의 70%까지 따른다.
- 우유거품을 조금 올린 뒤 휘핑크림을 올린다.
- 초코파우더와 초코소스로 토핑을 한다.

Type of glass

Santa ice glass
산타 아이스잔

Equipment
메뉴 만드는 기구

Espresso machine, foam maker, milk spoon & cream whipper
에스프레소 머신 · 거품기 · 우유스푼 · 휘핑기

카페모카를 시원하게 즐기는 메뉴로 쌉쌀함과 달콤함이 적절히 어우러진 것이 특징이다.

Follow the Steps
▶▶| 만드는 순서

❶

❷

❸

❹

❺

❻

# 05. Iced Coffee Menus

## Iced Caramel Macchiato
아이스 캐러멜 마끼아또

This is the cold menu of caramel macchiato, which is recommended if you want to enjoy a sweet and refreshing coffee beverage during the summer.

**Ingredients**
재료

- Whole beans for espresso, caramel syrup, milk, ice, and caramel sauce
- 에스프레소용 원두, 캐러멜시럽, 우유, 얼음, 캐러멜소스

**How to Make**
만드는 방법

- Fill the ice glass with ice. Put 2 cameral sauce pumps to the glass.
- Pour milk up to 70% of the glass.
- Brew 2 shots of espresso, and pour it to the glass.
- Add a little milk foam on top.
- Add caramel sauce as a topping.

- 아이스잔에 얼음을 채운 후 캐러멜시럽 2펌핑을 한다.
- 우유를 잔의 70%까지 붓는다.
- 에스프레소 2샷을 추출하여 아이스잔에 붓는다.
- 우유거품을 올린다.
- 캐러멜소스로 토핑을 한다.

Type of glass

Santa ice glass
산타 아이스잔

Equipment
메뉴 만드는 기구

Espresso machine, foam maker & milk spoon
에스프레소 머신 · 거품기 · 우유스푼

캐러멜 마끼아또를 차갑게 만든 커피메뉴로 여름철 달콤한 커피 음료로 추천할 만하다.

Follow the Steps
▶▶| 만드는 순서

❶

❷

❸

❹

❺

❻

# 05. Iced Coffee Menus

## Espresso Shakerrato
## 에스프레소 샤커레또

Shakerrato, meaning 'to shake,' is an Italian traditional beverage. The layers created by coffee and affluent foam result in a luxurious presentation.

| Ingredients<br>재료 | • Whole beans for espresso, sugar, and ice<br>• 에스프레소용 원두, 설탕, 얼음 |
|---|---|
| How to Make<br>만드는 방법 | • Brew 3 shots of espresso.<br>• Put 15 grams of sugar, 7 to 8 ice cubes, and 3 shots of espresso in the shaker. Shake it to mix the ingredients all together.<br>• Pour the mixture to the wine glass. Decorate the top with 2 to 3 whole beans.<br>• 에스프레소 3샷을 추출한다.<br>• 셰이커에 설탕 15g, 얼음 7~8개, 에스프레소 3샷을 넣고 셰이킹을 한다.<br>• 와인잔에 따른 후 원두 2~3알로 토핑을 한다. |

Type of glass

Wine glass
와인잔

Equipment
메뉴 만드는 기구

Espresso machine & shaker
에스프레소 머신 · 셰이커

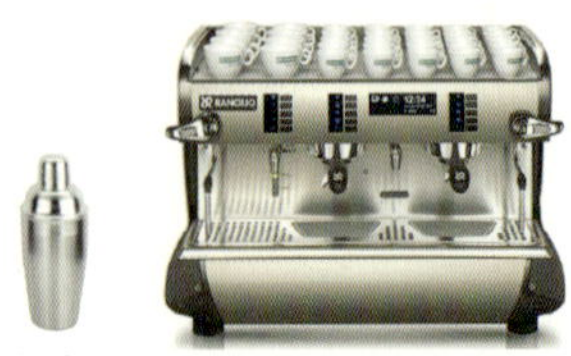

샤커레또 (Shakerrato)는 이탈리아 전통 음료로 '흔들다'는 뜻이다. 커피와 풍부한 거품이 층을 이루고 있어 고급스러운 분위기를 풍긴다.

Follow the Steps
▶▶| 만드는 순서

❶

❷

❸

❹

❺

❻

# 05. Iced Coffee Menus

## Espresso Freddo
## 에스프레소 프레도

The freshly brewed espresso which is poured into the straight glass is able to keep the unique flavors of espresso. If you put into the brewed espresso, the coffee will easily lose its flavors as the ice melts.

| | |
|---|---|
| Ingredients<br>재료 | • Whole beans for espresso, and ice<br>• 에스프레소용 원두, 얼음 |
| How to Make<br>만드는 방법 | • Put crushed ice in the ice bowl and plant the straight glass in the ice.<br>• Brew 1 shot of espresso, and pour it into the straight glass.<br>• 아이스볼에 분쇄된 얼음을 담고 스트레이트잔을 꽂는다.<br>• 에스프레소 1샷을 스텐샷에 추출하여 스트레이트잔에 붓는다. |

Type of glass

Small ice bowl & straight glass
소형 아이스 볼 · 스트레이트잔

Equipment
메뉴 만드는 기구

Espresso machine
에스프레소 머신

갓내린 에스프레소를 얼음 속에 둔 차가운 잔에 부어 급냉한 음료로 에스프레소의 향미를 유지한 상태에서 연해지지 않고 시원하게 마실 수 있는 메뉴이다.

Follow the Steps
**만드는 순서**

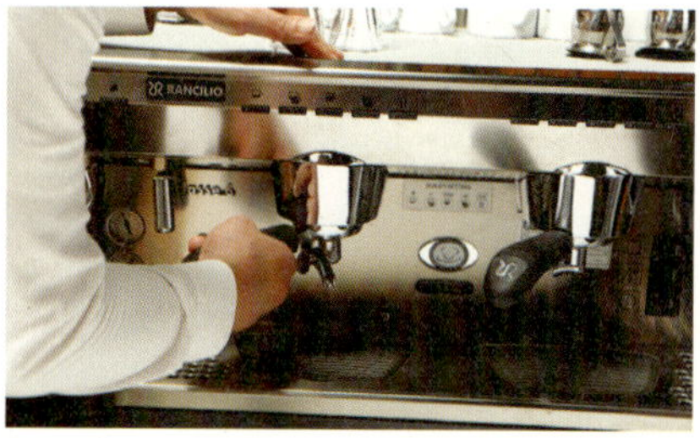

❶

❷

❸

❹

❺

❻

# 05. Iced Coffee Menus

## Iced Café Vienna
## 아이스 카페 비엔나

Whipped cream added to iced americano provides a sweet and light finishing touch to this menu.

| | |
|---|---|
| Ingredients<br>재료 | • Whole beans for espresso, water, ice, sugar syrup, and whipped cream<br>• 에스프레소용 원두, 차가운 물, 얼음, 설탕 시럽, 휘핑크림 |
| How to Make<br>만드는 방법 | • Fill the wine glass with ice. Put 2 sugar syrup pumps to the glass.<br>• Fill70% of the glass with cold water.<br>• Brew 2 shots of espresso, and pour it to the glass.<br>• Add whipped cream on top.<br>• 와인잔에 얼음을 채운 후 설탕시럽 2펌핑을 한다.<br>• 차가운 물을 잔의 70%까지 붓는다.<br>• 에스프레소 2샷을 추출하여 와인잔에 붓는다.<br>• 휘핑크림을 올린다. |

Type of glass

Wine glass
와인 잔

Equipment
메뉴 만드는 기구

Espresso machine & cream whipper
에스프레소 머신 · 휘핑기

아이스 아메리카노에 휘핑크림이 올라간 메뉴로 생크림의 달콤함이 가볍게 마무리 해준다.

Follow the Steps
▶▶| 만드는 순서

❶

❷

❸

❹

❺

❻

# 05. Iced Coffee Menus

## Double Iced Coffee
## 더블 아이스 커피

This menu has neat and strong flavors created by ice cubes made of frozen drip coffee and espresso. The ice cubes made of coffee also has an effect to maintain the coffee's flavors for a long time.

**Ingredients**
재료

- Ice cubes made of Rosa blend coffee whole beans for espresso, ice, and cold water

- 로사 블렌딩 커피로 만든 얼음, 에스프레소용 원두, 얼음, 차가운 물

**How to Make**
만드는 방법

- Put 10 ice cubes made of Rosa coffee to the ice glass. Fill the rest with normal ice cubes.
- Fill 80% of the glass with cold water.
- Brew 2 shots of espresso, and pour it to the glass.

- 아이스잔에 로사커피로 얼린 얼음 10개를 넣고, 부족한 양 만큼 일반 얼음으로 가득 채운다.
- 차가운 물을 잔의 80%까지 붓는다.
- 에스프레소 2샷을 추출하여 잔에 붓는다.

Type of glass

Ice glass
아이스잔

Equipment
메뉴 만드는 기구

Espresso machine
에스프레소 머신

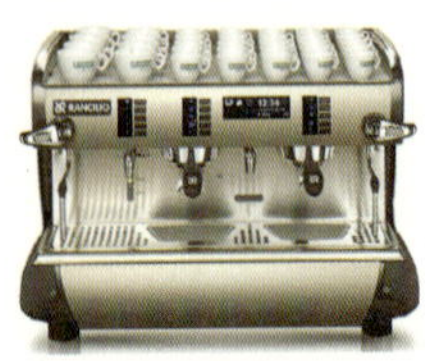

얼려진 드립커피에 에스프레소를 넣어 깔끔하고 진한 커피가 함께 어우러진 맛을 내며 특히 시간이 지나도 커피맛의 변화가 적다.

Follow the Steps
▶▶| 만드는 순서

❶

❷

❸

❹

❺

❻

# 05. Iced Coffee Menus

## Affogato
## 아포가토

'Affogato'means 'drowned' in Italian. This sweet dessert menu is enjoyed by topping espresso on ice cream.

**Ingredients**
**재료**

- Whole beans for espresso, vanilla ice cream, and chocolate sauce
- 에스프레소용 원두, 바닐라 아이스크림, 초코소스

**How to Make**
**만드는 방법**

- Put 1 and ½ scoops of ice cream to the affogato glass.
- Pour 2 shots of ristretto. Add chocolate sauce on top.
  - You may want to caramel or chocolate sauce according to your preference.

- 아포가토 잔에 아이스크림 1과 1/2 스쿱을 담는다.
- 리스트레또 2샷을 붓고 초코소스로 토핑을 한다.
  ※취향에 따라 캐러멜소스나 초콜릿소스를 토핑하여 즐겨도 좋다.

Type of glass

Affogato glass
아포가토 잔

Equipment
메뉴 만드는 기구

Espresso machine & ice cream scoop
에스프레소 머신 · 아이스크림 스쿱

아포가토(Affogato)는 이탈리아 어로 '끼얹다', '빠지다' 라는 뜻으로 아이스크림에 에스프레소를 끼얹어 즐기는 달콤한 디저트 메뉴이다.

Follow the Steps
▶▶| 만드는 순서

❶

❷

❸

❹

❺

❻

## Green Tea Affogato
## 그린 티 아포가토

This menu adds green tea latte instead of espresso to ice cream, providing nutty and bitter tastes and flavors of green tea.

**Ingredients**
재료

- Green tea ice bream, steamed milk, and green tea powder
- 녹차 아이스크림, 스팀우유, 녹차파우더

**How to Make**
만드는 방법

- Measure 10 grams of green tea powder and 30 ml of milk. Mix them well together.
- Put 1 and ½ scoops of ice cream in the affogato glass.
- Pour green tea latte into the affogato glass. Add green tea powder as a topping.

- 계량컵에 녹차파우더 10g과 스팀우유 30ml를 넣고 잘 섞어준다.
- 아포가토잔에 아이스크림 1과 1/2스쿱을 담는다.
- 녹차라떼를 아포가토잔에 부은 후 녹차파우더로 토핑한다.

Type of glass

Affogato glass
아포가토 잔

Equipment
메뉴 만드는 기구

Measuring cup & ice cream scoop
계량컵 · 아이스크림 스쿱

아이스크림에 에스프레소 대신 녹차라떼를 끼얹은 아포가토로
녹차의 고소하고 쌉살한 맛과 향을 즐길 수 있다.

Follow the Steps
▶▶| 만드는 순서

❶

❷

❸

❹

❺

❻

Aida
Terrassen
Kaffee
CAFÉ KONDITOREI
PROUSEK & CO
COFFEE TO GO

# 06
# Santaccino

# 06. Santaccino

## Espresso Santaccino
## 에스프레소 산타치노

This slush is made by mixing a strong espresso, milk, and ice all together. It has a gentle vanilla flavor.

**Ingredients**
재료

- Whole beans for espresso, milk, vanilla powder, ice, and whipped cream
- 에스프레소용 원두, 우유, 바닐라파우더, 얼음, 휘핑크림

**How to Make**
만드는 방법

- Put 12 to 13 ice cubes, 24 grams of vanilla powder, and 20 ml of milk yogurt in the blender bowl.
- Brew 4 shots of ristretto. Add it to the bowl and mix it with other ingredients.
- Pour the mixture to the glass. Add whipped cream on top. Put 2 to 3 whole beans for decoration.

- 블렌더 볼에 얼음 12~13개와 바닐라파우더 24g과 우유 20ml를 넣는다.
- 리스트레또 4샷을 추출한 후 블렌더 볼에 넣고 함께 믹스한다.
- 잔에 따른 뒤 휘핑크림을 올리고 원두 2~3알로 토핑을 한다.

Type of glass

Santa ice glass
산타 아이스잔

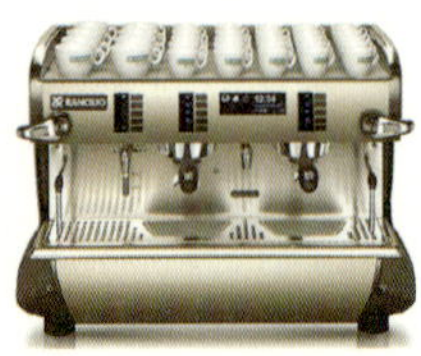

Equipment
메뉴 만드는 기구

Espresso machine, blender & cream whipper
에스프레소 머신 · 블렌더 · 휘핑기

진한 에스프레소와 우유, 얼음을 블렌더로 믹스하여 만든 슬러쉬(Slush), 은은한 바닐라 향이 좋은 메뉴이다.

Follow the Steps
▶▶| 만드는 순서

❶

❷

❸

❹

❺

❻

# 06. Santaccino

## Caramel Vanilla Santaccino
캐러멜 바닐라 산타치노

This slush menu presents a balance between the strong flavor of espresso and the soft and fragrant flavors of vanilla powder and caramel sauce.

**Ingredients**
재료

- Whole beans for espresso, milk, caramel sauce, vanilla powder, ice, and whipped cream
- 에스프레소용 원두, 우유, 캐러멜소스, 바닐라파우더, 얼음, 휘핑크림

**How to Make**
만드는 방법

- Put 12 to 13 ice cubes, 24 grams of vanilla powder, 50 ml of milk, and 1 and ½ caramel sauce pumps in the blender bowl.
- Brew 2 shots of espresso. Add it to the bowl and mix it with other ingredients.
- Pour the mixture to the ice glass. Add whipped cream on to. Drizzle caramel sauce.

- 블렌더 볼에 얼음 12~13개와 바닐라파우더 24g, 우유 50ml를 붓고 캐러멜소스 1과 1/2 펌핑을 넣는다.
- 에스프레소 2샷을 추출한 후 블렌더 볼에 넣고 함께 믹스한다.
- 아이스잔에 따른 뒤 휘핑크림을 올리고 캐러멜소스로 토핑을 한다.

Type of glass

Santa ice glass
산타 아이스잔

Equipment
메뉴 만드는 기구

Espresso machine, blender & cream whipper
에스프레소 머신 · 블렌더 · 휘핑기

에스프레소에 부드러운 바닐라, 향긋한 캐러멜의 조화를 맛볼 수 있는 슬러쉬 메뉴이다.

Follow the Steps
▶▶| 만드는 순서

❶

❷

❸

❹

❺

❻

# 06. Santaccino

## Mint Chocolate Santaccino
## 민트초코 산타치노

This slush menu has sweet chocolate and refreshing mint flavors.

### Ingredients
재료

- Whole beans for espresso, milk, mint syrup, mint chocolate powder, whipped cream, and chocolate powder
- 에스프레소용 원두, 우유, 민트시럽, 민트초코파우더, 얼음, 휘핑크림, 초콜릿파우더

### How to Make
만드는 방법

- Put 12 to 13 ice cubes, 2 mint syrup pumps, 25 grams of mint chocolate powder, and 50ml of milk in the blender bowl.
- Brew 2 shots of espresso. Add it to the bowl and mix it with other ingredients.
- Pour the mixture to the ice glass. Add whipped cream on to. Decorate with chocolate powder and mint syrup.

- 블렌더 볼에 얼음 12~13개와 민트시럽 2펌핑을 하고 민트초코파우더 25g, 우유 50ml를 넣는다.
- 에스프레소 2샷을 추출한 후 블렌더 볼에 넣고 함께 믹스한다.
- 아이스잔에 따른 후 휘핑크림을 올리고 초코파우더와 민트시럽으로 토핑한다.

Type of glass

Santa ice glass
산타 아이스잔

Equipment
메뉴 만드는 기구

Espresso machine, blender & cream whipper
에스프레소 머신 · 블렌더 · 휘핑기

달콤한 초콜릿 맛과 상쾌한 민트향이 함께 어우러진 슬러쉬 메뉴이다.

Follow the Steps
▶▶| 만드는 순서

❶

❷

❸

❹

❺

❻

# 06. Santaccino

## Mocha Santaccino
## 모카 산타치노

This slush menu combines the strong flavors of dark chocolate and espresso.

| | |
|---|---|
| Ingredients<br>재료 | • Whole beans for espresso, milk, chocolate sauce, mochaccino powder, ice, whipped cream, and chocolate powder<br>• 에스프레소용 원두, 우유, 초코소스, 모카치노파우더, 얼음, 휘핑크림, 초코파우더 |
| How to Make<br>만드는 방법 | • Put 12 to 13 ice cubes, 1 and ½ chocolate sauce pumps, 35 grams of mochaccino powder, and 50 ml of milk in the blender bowl. Mix them together.<br>• Brew 2 shots of espresso. Add it to the bowl and mix it with other ingredients.<br>• Pour the mixture to the ice glass. Add whipped cream on to. Decorate with chocolate sauce and powder.<br>• 블렌더 볼에 얼음 12~13개와 초코소스 1과 1/2 펌핑을 하고 모카치노파우더 35g과 우유 50ml를 넣는다.<br>• 에스프레소 2샷을 추출한 후 블렌더 볼에 넣고 함께 믹스한다.<br>• 아이스잔에 따른 뒤 휘핑크림을 올리고 초코소스와 초코파우더로 토핑을 한다. |

Type of glass

Santa ice glass
산타 아이스잔

Equipment
메뉴 만드는 기구

Espresso machine, blender & cream whipper
에스프레소 머신 · 블렌더 · 휘핑기

진한 초콜릿의 맛이 에스프레소와 어우러진 슬러쉬 메뉴이다.

Follow the Steps
▶▶| 만드는 순서

❶

❷

❸

❹

❺

❻

# 06. Santaccino

## Java Chip Santaccino
## 자바칩 산타치노

This slush menu presents an interesting harmony between the bitter sweet taste of chocolate and fun chewing texture of Java chips.

**Ingredients**
**재료**

- Whole beans for espresso, milk, Java chip powder, ice, whipped cream, and chocolate powder
- 에스프레소용 원두, 우유, 자바칩파우더, 얼음, 휘핑크림, 초코파우더

**How to Make**
**만드는 방법**

- Put 12 to 13 ice cubes, 60 grams of Java chip powder, and 125 ml of milk in the blender bowl. Mix them together.
- Pour the mixture to the ice glass. Add whipped cream on top. Sprinkle chocolate powder as a topping.
  – You may want to add 1 shot of espresso according to your preference.
- 블렌더 볼에 얼음 12~13개와 자바칩파우더 60g, 우유 125ml을 넣고 믹스한다.
- 아이스잔에 따른 뒤 휘핑크림을 올리고 초코파우더로 토핑을 한다.
  ※기호에 따라 에스프레소 1샷을 추가할 수 있다.

Type of glass

Santa ice glass
산타 아이스잔

Equipment
메뉴 만드는 기구

Espresso machine, blender & cream whipper
에스프레소 머신 · 블렌더 · 휘핑기

초콜릿의 달콤쌉살한 맛과 자바칩의 씹히는 맛이 어우러져 재미를 선사하는 슬러쉬 메뉴이다.

Follow the Steps
▶▶| 만드는 순서

❶

❷

❸

❹

❺

❻

# 06. Santaccino

## Green Tea Santaccino
그린 티 산타치노

This slush menu presents the exciting moment to enjoy the strong and unique flavor of green tea with the soft and sweet texture of milk and whipped cream.

### Ingredients
재료

- Milk, green tea powder, ice, and whipped cream
- 우유, 녹차파우더, 얼음, 휘핑크림

### How to Make
만드는 방법

- Put 12 to 13 ice cubes, 50 grams of green tea powder, and 125 ml of milk in the blender bowl. Mix them together.
- Pour the mixture to the ice glass. Add whipped cream on top. Sprinkle green tea powder as a topping.

- 블렌더 볼에 얼음 12~13개와 녹차파우더 50g, 우유 125ml을 넣고 믹스한다.
- 아이스잔에 따른 뒤 휘핑크림을 올리고 녹차파우더로 토핑을 한다.

Type of glass

Santa ice glass
산타 아이스잔

Equipment
메뉴 만드는 기구

Blender & cream whipper
블렌더 · 휘핑기

진한 녹차 특유의 향을 부드럽고 달콤하게 즐길 수 있는 슬러쉬 메뉴이다.

Follow the Steps
▶▶| 만드는 순서

❶

❷

❸

❹

❺

❻

# 07
# Smoothies

# 07. Smoothies

## Yoghurt Smoothie
## 요거트 스무디

This cold but soft menu provides a variety of tastes and pleasing presentation by effectively displaying the blended ice and fresh fruits and other refreshing toppings.

| Ingredients<br>재료 | • Plain yogurt, milk, yogurt powder, and ice<br>• 플레인 요거트, 우유, 요거트파우더, 얼음, 토핑용 과일, 휘핑크림 |
|---|---|
| How to Make<br>만드는 방법 | • Put 12 to 13 ice cubes, 100 ml of yogurt, 40 grams of yogurt powder, and 50 ml of milk in the blender bowl.<br>• Pour the mixture to the yogurt glass, and decorate with fruits and whipped cream.<br>• 블렌더 볼에 얼음 12~13개와 플레인 요거트 100ml, 요거트파우더 40g, 우유 50ml를 넣고 믹스한다.<br>• 요거트잔에 따른 후 과일과 휘핑크림으로 토핑한다. |

Type of glass

Yogurt glass
요거트 잔

Equipment
메뉴 만드는 기구

Blender
블렌더

플레인 요거트를 얼음과 신선한 과일 등을 함께 블렌더로 믹스한 음료에 여러 가지 과일을 토핑한 부드럽고 차가운 음료이다.

Follow the Steps
▶▶| 만드는 순서

❶

❷

❸

❹

❺

❻

# 07. Smoothies

## Strawberry Banana Smoothie
## 딸기 바나나 스무디

This menu presents a pleasing harmony between the refreshing flavor of strawberries, and the soft texture of bananas and yogurt.

**Ingredients**
재료

- Plain yogurt, strawberry smoothie juice, banana, and ice
- 플레인 요거트, 딸기 스무디 원액, 바나나, 얼음

**How to Make**
만드는 방법

- Put 12 to 13 ice cubes, 100 ml of plain yogurt, 100 ml of strawberry smoothie concentrate, and ½ banana in the blender bowl.
- Pour the mixture to the ice glass.
- 블렌더 볼에 얼음 12~13개와 플레인 요거트 100ml, 딸기 스무디 원액 100ml, 바나나 1/2개를 넣고 믹스한다.
- 아이스잔에 따른다.

Type of glass

Santa ice glass
산타 아이스잔

Equipment
메뉴 만드는 기구

Blender
블렌더

상큼한 딸기향과 부드러운 바나나의 질감이 요거트와 잘 어우러진 메뉴이다.

Follow the Steps
▶▶I 만드는 순서

❶

❷

❸

❹

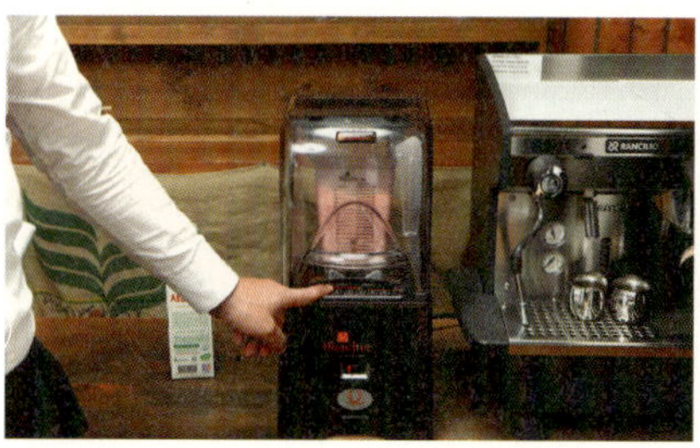
❺

❻

# 07. Smoothies

## Mixed Berry Smoothie
## 믹스 베리 스무디

This menu presents a refreshing taste created by the combination of smoothe concentrate, including acai berries, blueberries, and pomegranates, and yogurt.

| Ingredients<br>재료 | • Plain yogurt, mixed-berry smoothie, and ice<br>• 플레인 요거트, 믹스 베리 스무디 원액, 얼음 |
|---|---|
| How to Make<br>만드는 방법 | • Put 12 to 13 ice cubes, 100 ml of plain yogurt, and 100 ml of mixed berry smoothie concentrate in the blender bowl.<br>• Pour the mixture to the ice glass.<br>• 블렌더 볼에 얼음 12~13개와 플레인 요거트 100ml, 믹스베리 스무디 원액 100ml를 넣고 믹스한다.<br>• 아이스잔에 따른다. |

Type of glass

Santa ice glass
산타 아이스잔

Equipment 메뉴 만드는 기구 | Blender 블렌더

아사이베리, 블루베리, 석류가 첨가된 스무디 원액과 요거트를 믹스한 상큼한 맛이 조화를 이룬다.

Follow the Steps
▶▶| 만드는 순서

❶

❷

❸

❹

❺

❻

# 07. Smoothies

## Mulberry Smoothie
## 오디 스무디

Mixing mulberry concentrate with yogurt, this menu provides customers with satisfaction both in taste and health.

| | |
|---|---|
| Ingredients<br>재료 | • Mulberry juice, ice, and plain yogurt<br>• 오디원액, 얼음, 플레인 요거트 |
| How to Make<br>만드는 방법 | • Put 12 to 13 ice cubes, 100 ml of plain yogurt, and 75 ml of mulberries in the blender bowl.<br>• Pour the mixture to the ice glass.<br>• 블렌더 볼에 얼음 12~13개와 플레인 요거트 100ml 그리고 오디원액 75ml를 함께 넣고 믹스를 한다.<br>• 아이스잔에 따른다. |

Type of glass

Santa ice glass
산타 아이스잔

Equipment
메뉴 만드는 기구

Blender
블렌더

요거트에 오디 원액을 함께 믹스하여 맛과 건강까지 챙긴 음료이다.

Follow the Steps

▶▶| 만드는 순서

❶

❷

❸

❹

❺

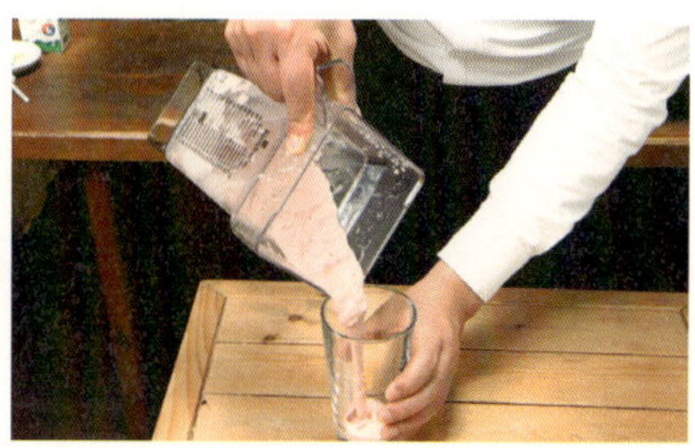

❻

# 07. Smoothies

## Mango Banana Smoothie
## 망고 바나나 스무디

This menu, which mixes mango smoothie concentrate, banana, and ice, has a pleasing harmony between the sweetness of the mango and the refreshing feeling of yogurt.

**Ingredients**
**재료**

- Plain yogurt, mango smoothie juice, banana, and ice
- 플레인 요거트, 망고 스무디 원액, 바나나, 얼음

**How to Make**
**만드는 방법**

- Put 12 to 13 ice cubes, 100 ml of yogurt, 100 ml of mango smoothie concentrate, and ½ banana in the blender bowl.
- Pour the mixture to the ice glass.

- 블렌더 볼에 얼음 12~13개와 플레인 요거트 100ml, 망고 스무디 원액 100ml, 바나나 1/2개를 넣고 믹스한다.
- 아이스잔에 따른다.

Type of glass

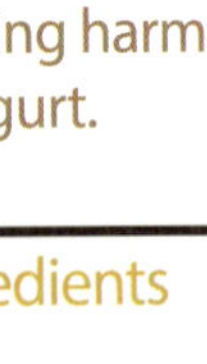

Santa ice glass
산타 아이스잔

Equipment
메뉴 만드는 기구

Blender
블렌더

요거트에 망고스무디원액과 바나나, 얼음을 함께 믹스한 것으로
달콤한 망고와 요거트의 새콤함이 느껴지는 메뉴이다.

Follow the Steps
▶▶| 만드는 순서

❶

❷

❸

❹

❺

❻

# 08
# Other Menus

# 08. Other Menus

## Green Tea Latte
## 녹차라떼

In this menu, which consists of green tea powder and milk, the astringent taste of green tea powder is relieved by milk.

| | |
|---|---|
| Ingredients<br>재료 | • Green tea powder and steamed milk<br>• 녹차파우더, 스팀우유 |
| How to Make<br>만드는 방법 | Use a Santa tea cup<br>• Put 15 grams of green tea powder in the tea cup.<br>• Melt green tea powder with a little amount of steamed milk.<br>• Create your own latte art by pouring steamed milk to the tea cup.<br>산타 티잔 사용<br>• 티잔에 녹차파우더 15g을 넣는다.<br>• 스팀우유 소량으로 녹차파우더를 녹인다.<br>• 스팀우유를 이용하여 티잔에 따르면서 아트를 그린다. |

Type of glass

Santa tea cup
산타 티잔

Equipment
메뉴 만드는 기구

Espresso machine & steam pitcher
에스프레소 머신 · 스팀피처

녹차파우더와 우유로 만든 음료로써 녹차의 쌉살함을 우유가 부드럽게 감싸준다.

Follow the Steps
▶▶| 만드는 순서

❶

❷

❸

❹

❺

❻

# 08. Other Menus

## How to Make
만드는 방법

### Use a Santa latte cup
- Put 20 grams of green tea powder to a Santa latte cup.
- Melt green tea powder using a little amount of steamed milk.
- Create your own latter art by pouring steamed milk to the latte cup.

### 산타 라떼잔 사용
- 라떼잔에 녹차파우더 20g을 넣는다.
- 스팀우유 소량으로 녹차파우더를 녹인다.
- 스팀우유를 이용하여 라떼잔에 따르면서 아트를 그린다.

Type of glass

Santa latte cup
산타 라떼잔

Follow the Steps
▶▶| 만드는 순서

❶

❷

❸

❹

❺

❻

# 08. Other Menus

## Iced Tea Latte
## 아이스 녹차라떼

The combination of cold milk and green tea powder creates a harmony between the refreshing feeling and nutty flavor of green tea powder in this menu.

**Ingredients**
재료

- Green tea powder, milk, and ice

- 녹차파우더, 우유, 얼음

**How to Make**
만드는 방법

- Fill an ice glass with ice.
- Measure 180 ml of milk and 40 grams of green tea powder using a measuring cup. Mix them together.
- Pour the mixture to the ice glass.
- Add milk foam on top. Sprinkle green tea powder as a topping.

- 아이스잔에 얼음을 채운다.
- 계량컵에 우유 180ml와 녹차파우더 40g을 넣어 혼합한다.
- 아이스잔에 따른다.
- 우유거품을 올린 후 녹차파우더로 토핑을 한다.

Type of glass

Santa ice glass
산타 아이스잔

Equipment
메뉴 만드는 기구

Measuring cup, hand mixer, foam maker & milk spoon
계량컵 · 핸드믹서기 · 거품기 · 우유스푼

차가운 우유에 녹차파우더를 녹여 시원하게 마시는 음료로써 차가운 얼음과 고소한 녹차의 풍미가 잘 어우러진다.

Follow the Steps
▶▶| 만드는 순서

❶

❷

❸

❹

❺

❻

# 08. Other Menus

## Chocolate Latte Original
## 초코라떼 오리지널

As the dark chocolate melts in the milk, this menu has a strong chocolate flavor and sweetness filling and lingering in the mouth.

| | |
|---|---|
| **Ingredients**<br>재료 | • Couverture chocolate and milk<br>• 커버추어 초콜릿, 우유 |
| **How to Make**<br>만드는 방법 | • Pour 100 ml of milk to a steam pitcher.<br>• Add 45 pieces of coverture chocolate, and boil it on the induction cooker, constantly stirring.<br>• Pour it to the cappuccino cup.<br>• 스팀피쳐에 우유 100ml을 붓는다.<br>• 커버추어 초콜릿 45개를 넣고, 인덕션으로 가열하여 저어가며 녹인다.<br>• 카푸치노잔에 따른다. |

Type of glass

Santa cappuccinp cup
산타 카푸치노잔

Equipment
메뉴 만드는 기구

Steam pitcher & induction cooker
스팀피처 · 인덕션

진한 다크 초콜릿을 직접 우유에 넣어 가열하여 녹인 메뉴로 진한 초콜릿의 향과 입안 가득히 느껴지는 달콤함이 특징이다.

Follow the Steps
▶▶| 만드는 순서

❶

❷

❸

❹

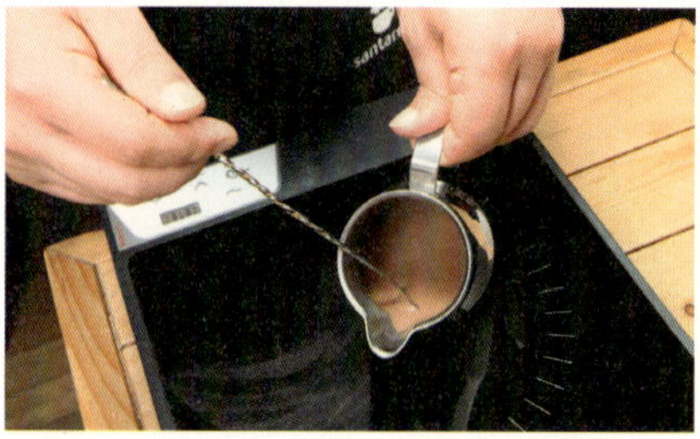
❺

❻

# 09
# Tea & Juice

# 09. Tea & Juice

## Home-made Lemon Tea
## 홈메이드 레몬티

With its high vitamin C, lemons are helpful for relaxation and skin care. In addition to these effects, this menu hasthefresh fragrance of lemons.

| | |
|---|---|
| Ingredients<br>재료 | • Sugar syrup, hot water, lemon juice, and lemon matured in sugar<br>• 설탕시럽, 뜨거운 물, 생 레몬, 레몬청 |
| How to Make<br>만드는 방법 | • Put 100 ml water, and 2 sugar syrup pumps to a steam pitcher.<br>• Add matured lemon in honey (lemon 0.5T / honey 0.5T).<br>• Squeeze juice form ½ lemon, and boil it.<br>• Pour the boiled beverage to the tea cup.<br>• 스팀피처에 물 100ml, 설탕시럽을 2펌핑을 한다.<br>• 레몬청(건더기 0.5T, 국물 0.5T)을 넣는다.<br>• 생 레몬 1/2을 즙을 내어서 넣고 가열한다.<br>• 가열 후에 티잔에 따른다. |

Type of glass

Santa tea cup
산타 티잔

Equipment
메뉴 만드는 기구

lemon squeezer, steam pitcher & induction cooker
레몬 스퀴저 · 스팀피처 · 인덕션

비타민C가 풍부하여 피로회복에도 도움이 되고 피부미용에도 좋은 레몬이 향긋하게 우러진 음료이다.

Follow the Steps

▶▶| 만드는 순서

❶

❷

❸

❹

❺

❻

## Iced Lemon Tea
## 아이스 레몬티

The refreshing feeling created by sour lemon and cold ice, makes it as one of the best summer beverages.

### Ingredients
### 재료

- Sugar syrup, lemon juice, lemon matured in sugar, water, and ice
- 설탕시럽, 생 레몬, 레몬청, 차가운 물, 얼음

### How to Make
### 만드는 방법

- Fill an ice glass with ice.
- Add 4 sugar syrup pumps, matured lemon in honey (lemon 1T / honey 1T), and lemon juice squeezed from 1 lemon to the glass.
- Pour cold water and mix it well.

- 아이스잔에 얼음을 채운다.
- 설탕시럽 4펌핑을 하고, 레몬청(건더기 1T, 국물 1T)과 생 레몬 1개를 즙을 내어 넣는다.
- 차가운 물을 붓고 혼합한다.

Type of glass

Santa ice glass
산타 아이스잔

Equipment
메뉴 만드는 기구

lemon squeezer
레몬 스퀴저

레몬의 상큼함과 시원함이 차가운 얼음을 만나 더욱 청량감을 주는 메뉴로서 여름철 갈증 해소 음료로도 좋다.

Follow the Steps
▶▶| 만드는 순서

❶

❷

❸

❹

❺

❻

## Tomato Juice
## 토마토 주스

Tomatoes have a high beta-carotene and lycopene content. It is reported that beta-carotene is good for eyesight, and lycopene has an excellent anti-tumor effect.

**Ingredients**
재료

- Tomato, water, sugar syrup, and ice
- 토마토, 차가운 물, 설탕시럽, 얼음

**How to Make**
만드는 방법

- Put 6 ice cubes, 160 grams of cherry tomatoes, 40 ml cold water, and 2 sugar syrup pumps in a blender bowl. Mix them all.
- Pour it to the ice glass.
- 블렌더 볼에 얼음 6개와 방울토마토 160g과 차가운 물 40ml, 설탕시럽 2와 1/2 펌핑을 하여 함께 믹스한다.
- 아이스잔에 따른다.

Type of glass

Santa ice glass
산타 아이스잔

Equipment
메뉴 만드는 기구

blender
블렌더

토마토의 베타 카로틴은 눈건강에 좋으며, 라이코펜 성분으로 항암효과가 뛰어나다.

Follow the Steps

▶▶| 만드는 순서

❶

❷

❸

❹

❺

❻

## Kiwi Juice
## 키위 주스

Containing rich vitamins, calcium, folic acid, phosphorus, and other nutrients, kiwis have an excellent antioxidant effect, and also improve immunity.

| | |
|---|---|
| Ingredients<br>재료 | • Kiwi, water, sugar syrup, and ice<br>• 키위, 차가운 물, 설탕시럽, 얼음 |
| How to Make<br>만드는 방법 | • Put 6 ice cubes, 100 ml water, and 2 sugar syrup pumps in a blender bowl. Mix them all.<br>• Put 2 kiwis, and blend them again at a low level. (Be careful not to grind kiwi seeds.)<br>• Pour the mixture to the ice glass.<br>• 블렌더 볼에 얼음 6개와 물 100ml, 설탕시럽 2펌핑을 하여 함께 믹스한다.<br>• 키위 2개를 추가로 넣고 약하게 한 번 더 믹스한다. (키위 씨가 갈아지지 않도록 한다.)<br>• 아이스잔에 따른다. |

Type of glass

Santa ice glass
산타 아이스잔

Equipment 메뉴 만드는 기구: blender 블렌더

키위는 비타민, 칼슘, 엽산, 인 등의 영양소가 풍부하게 들어있으며 특히 항산화 효과와 성인병예방, 면역력 증진에 효과가 좋다.

Follow the Steps
▶▶| 만드는 순서

❶

❷

❸

❹

❺

❻

# 09. Tea & Juice

## Banana Juice
## 바나나 주스

Due to the banana's high magnesium content, this menu serves as refreshment, and also acts as anappetite suppressant due to its particular fragrance and antiaging.

| | |
|---|---|
| Ingredients<br>재료 | • Banana, milk, sugar syrup, and ice<br>• 바나나, 우유, 설탕시럽, 얼음 |
| How to Make<br>만드는 방법 | • Put 6 ice cubes, 1 banana, 100 ml milk, and 1 and ½ sugar syrup pumps in a blender bowl. Mix them all.<br>• Pour it to the ice glass.<br>• 블렌더 볼에 얼음 6개와 바나나 1개, 우유 100ml, 설탕시럽 1과 1/2 펌핑을 하여 함께 믹스한다.<br>• 아이스잔에 따른다. |

Type of glass

Santa ice glass
산타 아이스잔

Equipment
메뉴 만드는 기구

blender
블렌더

바나나에는 마그네슘이 많이 들어 있어 기분을 좋게 하며 특정한 향으로 식욕을 억제하는 효과도 주며 노화방지, 피부미용 등에 좋은 음료이다.

Follow the Steps
▶▶| 만드는 순서

❶

❷

❸

❹

❺

❻

Lay's

# 10
# Side Dishes

# 10. Side Dish

## Waffle
## 와플

A honey comb-shaped waffle is generally divided into American and Belgian waffles even though it shows a little differences among countries. As many coffee shops present their signature waffle menu, it has been recreated from numerous innovative trials.

Very Berry Waffle — 베리베리 와플

와플은 표면이 벌집 모양으로 된 빵의 한 종류로써 나라마다 조금씩 다른 특징이 있으나 크게 미국식 와플과 벨기에식 와플로 나뉜다. 요즘에는 각 카페마다 시그니처 메뉴의 하나로써 여러 가지 시도를 통해 수 없이 많은 종류의 사이드 디쉬로 재탄생 하고 있다.

Chocolate Waffle
초콜릿 와플

Fruit Waffle
과일 와플

# 10. Side Dish

## Ice Sherbet
## 빙수

It is said that ancient Chinese began to eat snow or ice added with honey or fruit juice around 3000 B.C. In the West, Alexander the Great provided his soldiers who were exhausted with honey, fruit, and milk, mixing it with snow from the top of a mountain.

Beary good Ice sherbet — 베리굿 빙수

고대 중국인들은 기원전 3000년 경부터 눈이나 얼음에 꿀이나 과즙을 섞어 먹었다고 한다. 서양에서는 알렉산더 대왕이 지친 병사들에게 산정상의 눈을 퍼와 꿀과 과일, 우유를 섞어 먹여 기운을 차리게 했다는 이야기가 있다.

# 10. Side Dish

## Cake
## 케익

Cake with a sweet balance of cream and bread has been beloved as a dessert that goes along well with coffee or black tea. Numerous kinds of cakes are enjoyed in the world.

크림과 빵이 어우러진 달콤한 케익은 커피나 홍차 등과 함께 디저트로 사랑받아 왔고 그 종류만 해도 셀 수 없을 정도로 종류가 다양하다.

Photo by Famille 파미유

## 10. Side Dish

### Bagel
베이글

Originating from Jewish people's traditional recipes, it is said that an Austrian king asked a Jewish baker to make bread in the shape of a stirrup, which is bugel in German. Bagels are made of flower, water, salt, and yeast with no egg, milk, or butter. Slightly toasted bagels are usually enjoyed with cream cheese.

약 2000년 전부터 유대인들이 만들던 빵으로 오스트리아 왕이 유대인 제과업자에게 등자 모양을 만들게 한 데서부터 시작되었다. 베이글이란 이름 또한 독일어로 등자를 뜻하는 뷔글(Bugel) 에서 유래되었다. 베이글은 달걀, 우유, 버터 등을 넣지 않고 밀가루, 물, 소금, 이스트 만으로 만든다. 살짝 구워 크림치즈를 발라 먹는다.

Photo by Famille 파미유

# 10. Side Dish

## Chocolate
## 초콜릿

Chocolate is made with cocoa mass, cocoa butter, and other ingredients. It is beloved for its unique flavor and sweetness.

초콜릿은 카카오를 원료로한 카카오 매스와 카카오 버터 등으로 만든다. 독특한 향과 달콤함으로 많은 사랑을 받아오고 있다.

Photo by cacao boom 카카오 봄

# 10. Side Dish

## Macaron
마카롱

A macaron is a meringue-based confection made with almond powder, egg whites, and sugar. Colorful macarons present an enjoyable texture with an interesting combination of smooth and crunchy shells and moist filling between the shells.The name is derived from the Italian word macarone, which means a good dough.

마카롱은 아몬드 가루, 달걀흰자, 설탕 등으로 만들어지는 고급 머랭과자이다. 알록달록 아름다운 색깔에 겉은 매끈하면서 바삭하고 속은 촉촉한 머랭이로 즐거운 식감을 준다. 처음에는 잘된 반죽이라는 뜻의 마카로네(Marcerone)라는 이름으로 불렸다.

Photo by Famille 파미유

# 10. Side Dish

## Ice Cream
## 아이스크림

There is no established story about the origin of ice cream, but it is said that the ancient Chinese began to make it with water buffalos' milk. Ice cream, a beloved dessert from all around the world, has been developed to many different types.

아이스크림의 기원은 고대 중국에서 물소젖을 이용하여 만들어 먹었다고 하나 확실한 정설은 없다. 각 나라에서 여러가지 형태로 발전하여 요즘은 전 세계적으로 사랑 받는 디저트 식품이다.

# 10. Side Dish

## Cookie
## 쿠키

A cookie is a sweet treat. Cookie dough is spread at a certain thickness, and often added with chocolate chips, dried fruit, and nuts. Cookies commonly have sweet tastes and crunchy textures to go along with coffee.

반죽을 일정한 두께로 펴서 찍어내거나 잘라서 구워 만든 과자의 한 종류로 초코칩, 말린 과일, 견과류 등과 함께 구워내기도 한다. 종류에 따라 약간의 차이가 있지만 바삭한 식감과 함께 달콤한 맛으로 커피와 잘 어울린다.

Photo by Famille 파미유

# Epilogue

I have traveled all around the world to study coffee. While visiting coffee farms in many countries, I could obtain living information on global coffee production. When I visited coffee shops in different countries, I could expand my knowledge on the culture of coffee from the staff's explanation of their house coffee. My heart is still with kind and generous people who welcome me from Korea at various coffee farms and coffee shops. Publishing this book, I would like to deliver my deep appreciation for them.

커피 공부를 위해 세계를 돌아다녔다.
각국의 커피농장에서 커피생산 현황과 생생한 정보를 접했으며
카페에서는 하우스 커피에 대한 아낌없는 설명을 들으며 커피문화를 더 넓게 이해 할 수 있었다. 커피가 있는 현장에서 한국의 이방인을 따뜻하게 맞이해 주고 보살펴 주신 많은 분들의 얼굴이 지금도 선하다.
이 책을 출판하면서 다시 한 번 그 분들에게 감사의 마음을 전한다.

## At the Myanmar Coffee Institute and coffee farm

미얀마(커피 연구소 및 커피농장)

## At the Kenya Coffee Institute, Masai Coffee and coffee mill

케냐(커피연구소 및 마사이 커피, 커피 Mill)

## At a coffee farm and CCT in Thailand

태국(커피농장 및 CCT)

## At the NAEB, Cyngugu, Coopak, and Rwashoscco in Rwanda

르완다(NAEB, Cyngugu, Coopak, Rwashoscco)

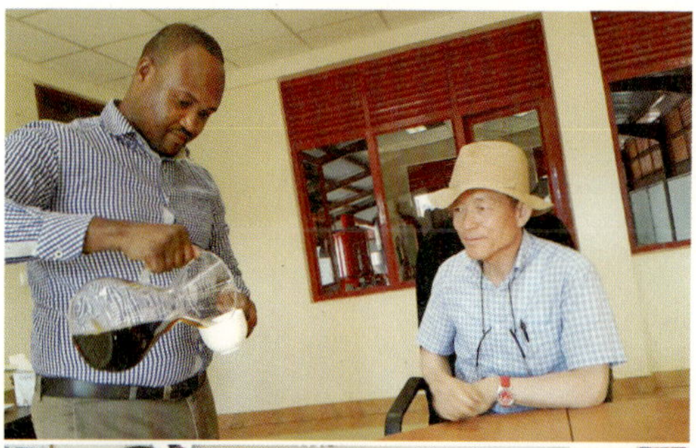

## At the Blawan Coffee farm and Coffee Institute in Indonesia

인도네시아(Blawan Coffee farm, Coffee 연구소)

## At the Coffee Association, Dalat coffee farm and Trung Nguyen Coffee in Vietnam

베트남(Coffee 조합, Dalat 커피농장, Trung Nguyen Coffee)

I also appreciate all the people who welcomed me and enriched my experiences at many coffee farms and cafes.

이 밖에 많은 커피농장과 카페에서 함께했던 분들에게도 감사를 전한다.

## References

자료참고

- http://blog.naver.com/mtop6874/10077760479 로리탐탐
- http://cafe.naver.com/coffeebasket/428 커피공화국
- www.piececake.co.kr 파미유
- cacao boom 카카오 봄